THREE SISTERS
IN A TIN HOUSE

*How We Survived the
Unimaginable and Unthinkable*

By J. S. Stone

Inspired Forever Book Publishing
Dallas, Texas

Three Sisters in a Tin House: How We Survived the Unimaginable and Unthinkable

Inspired Forever Book Publishing™
"Words with Lasting Impact"
Dallas, Texas
(214) 444-6062

Printed in the United States of America

Library of Congress Control Number: 2019910059

Softcover ISBN-13: 978-1-948903-20-2

Disclaimer: Any resemblance to actual persons, living or dead, or actual events is purely coincidental. I have tried to recreate events, locales, and conversations from my memories of them. In order to maintain their anonymity in some instances, I have changed the names of individuals and places, and may have changed some identifying characteristics and details such as physical properties, occupations, and places of residence.

DEDICATION

I dedicate this book to my sisters. We have been through more in life than most people go through in two lifetimes or more, yet the awful things we experienced and endured made us who we are today, and those things also made us stronger. The awful experiences we went through created a powerful bond between us. It's a stronger bond than any other sisters have together on this earth.

I also dedicate this story to my mother, who always did and still does the impossible and who somehow made and still makes everything okay, even when she was a victim of physical abuse for many years. She is a very strong woman today, with daughters and grandchildren who love her very much.

To my son, who grew up and became an awesome, smart, very loving, and very caring young man: You are working to make this world a better place. I thank God for you every day, son, and I will always love you to the moon and back, no matter how old you get.

To my nieces: Thank you to my oldest niece for helping me with this book, for helping me to make it a reality. I have watched you grow to become this amazing young woman who loves with no boundaries and goes out of her way to help everyone. You truly are an angel on earth. To my youngest niece: I have also watched you grow to become an amazing young woman, and like your cousin, you chose a career to help children. God bless y'all for that. I know you are both changing lives for the better every day. I am so proud of you both.

To my brother-in-law, who is more like a brother to me, thank you for being one of the kindest, most caring, and giving people I know.

And to my nephew: What a joy and blessing you have been to our family. I am so amazed at how smart you are. I am so proud of you too. I am very blessed to have such a beautiful family. I love you all very much.

And to all who have or are now experiencing domestic violence, may God bless you all from little to big. May God give you courage, strength, protection, and a voice with which to speak up and get help.

TABLE OF CONTENTS

PREFACE

Looking back upon my childhood, I can't decide if I was more frightened of our abusive father or of the ghost that was loud and merciless with its hauntings. Both presences terrified me and my two sisters, making an already unstable home life inescapably horrifying. As a child, I didn't fully understand the gravity of our father's mental volatility. I only knew that if he was drunk, violence could soon follow. The ghost, however, seemed to have no pattern, and would often make its presence known when the house was blissfully calm and quiet. Were we ever happy as a family? Of course. Were there pockets of normalcy? Absolutely. But it was hard to find joy in the highs when we never knew if the next low would be the last one we could survive. The ground was never steady beneath our feet, and that made for a miserable journey. Our only hope was to find strength in numbers and to somehow outlast both sources of terror. And that's exactly what we did.

The story I am about to tell is based on the true story of our childhood, to the best of our knowledge and collective memories. I know it wasn't easy for my mother and sisters to talk about those years in that little white tin house or the double-wide that replaced it. Unpacking all those feelings and experiences was a long, emotional process that, in the end, proved cathartic for all of us.

CHAPTER ONE

Where it All Began

Everyone has a story. This one is mine.

It all began on June 28, 1967. That was the day I was born. I arrived at 9:45 a.m. My mother and stepfather, Berry, were both young but very excited to begin their family. Mother had met Berry on the strip, a large shopping mall area where teens drove around aimlessly on weekend nights. Occasionally, they would park their cars so they could talk to their friends and meet new ones. Some of Mother's friends had introduced her to Berry. My mother said he was very handsome, and he seemed like a very nice young man. He was well-mannered and polite. Mother and Berry fell in love at first sight.

Mother was pregnant with me when she met Berry, but he did not mind that matter of fact. He accepted me as his child. My mother and my biological father, Johnny, were married briefly and only together for one week before Johnny was deployed by the navy. I was conceived during that one week, but they divorced shortly thereafter.

My mother started dating Berry as soon as her divorce was final, and Berry was at the hospital when I was born. Once we arrived home from the hospital, days and nights passed; I started to grow. I learned how to sit up, walk, and then talk. My first word was "sorsey," which was my way of saying, "horse." Yes, I loved horses.

Berry was enlisted in the army, so he was gone often. During those early years, my mother and I lived with Uncle Richard and Aunt Sue in Texas. They had a daughter, Debra, who was seven years older than I was. I don't have a lot of memories of living with them in Texas, except for one that still makes my family laugh to this day. I was around eighteen months old at the time. My mother, Uncle Richard, and Cousin Debra wanted to go see a movie. They took me with them. On the way back, I had fallen asleep in the back seat of the car, quiet as a mouse. Uncle Richard was driving, and my mother was in the passenger seat with Debra between them. They were discussing how good the movie was and couldn't wait to get home to tell Aunt Sue all about it. Uncle Richard pulled the car into the garage, and they all rushed into the house to find Aunt Sue. Debra reenacted scenes from the movie as the adults watched intently until Aunt Sue interrupted: "Where's Julie?"

In the meantime, I had woken up alone in the car in the dark garage. I stood up and touched the car door window in the back seat and started to cry. Aunt Sue opened the door to the garage and walked up to the car. She opened the car door and said, "There she is!" She picked me up and hugged me, all the while saying to me, "Poor baby; they left this poor baby out here all by herself in the dark." She walked back into the house with me. I stopped crying, and I looked at my mother, who had her arms outstretched for me. I reached my arms out to her also. My mother took me from Aunt Sue and held me, as I laid my head on her shoulder.

Not long after this, Uncle Richard accepted an offer for a better paying job in Oklahoma, so he and Aunt Sue bought a house there, and we moved with them. A long, one-lane sand road led to their new house, and the house itself sat back from the sand road and had its own long sand driveway. Tall trees surrounded the yard and house. It was a beautiful place located out in the country.

While living there with them, I would wake up to the smell of the delicious breakfast that my aunt Sue would make for my uncle Richard. I would sit up in bed and rub my little sleepy eyes. I would crawl out of bed and walk up to Uncle Richard, who was always sitting at the kitchen table. He would pick me up and put me in his lap. He would give me a bite of food and then take a bite himself. This was our routine every morning.

After breakfast, we would head outside to the back yard where the barn was located. They had a cow in a small pasture that also had access to the barn; chickens that ran everywhere in all directions all over the backyard; and pigs in a pigpen that Uncle Richard had built. For a pigpen, it sure was a fancy one. It had a little shed inside it that was just tall enough to allow the pigs to take shelter from the rain and storms or the hot sun. Every morning, Uncle Richard would feed the animals and let me help him some. I didn't mind throwing handfuls of chicken feed on the ground, but I was too scared to feed the pigs; they were big and scary looking to me. Last, we would go into the barn where the cow was waiting on her food. I would help Uncle Richard pour her feed into her trough.

After all the animals were fed, we would milk the cow. The cow did not mind at all. She would just stand there and eat her food while Uncle Richard put his little wooden stool beside her and a pail underneath her udders. He would sit down on the little wooden stool and rub his hands together before putting them on her udders and squeezing in a downward motion. The milk squirted out of her udders and into the large silver pail. When I got a little older, Uncle Richard let me milk the cow all by myself. In several minutes, the pail would be filled with warm white milk that had a thick creamy foam on top.

Uncle Richard and I would take the milk back to the house where Aunt Sue was waiting for us in the kitchen. She would have our drinking glasses lined up on the kitchen counter. "Here you go," Uncle Richard would always say, as he would lift up the pail of milk and sit it on the counter next to the drinking glasses. Aunt Sue would wipe the cream off the top of the milk and, using a measuring cup, she would dip each of us a glass of it. Nothing tasted better than a glass of fresh milk.

On their small farm they also had a Collie that looked just like Lassie. Her name was Stinker. I remember her long snout was always in my face, providing unsolicited kisses. One morning, Uncle Richard and Aunt Sue took me on a walk to the creek. It was a cool, crisp morning as we strolled along the creek bank. Uncle Richard and Aunt Sue kept a steady pace as Stinker and I followed closely behind. Eventually, my curious nature drew me closer to the creek's edge as my aunt and uncle carried on, not realizing I had stopped dangerously close to the water. I peered over the edge of the creek bank to look down at the gently flowing water, which sparkled in the morning sunlight. Stinker was by my side, and as my little feet inched closer to the edge, she began barking, warning my aunt and uncle to turn around. They were not far from me and moved quickly to scoop me up just before my curiosity got the best of me. Aunt Sue gently scolded me, saying, "You can't get close to the creek, Julie! You can fall into the water, and it will hurt you. It's a good thing Stinker barked when she did!" Yes, Stinker came to the rescue, just like Lassie. She saved me from falling into the creek that day.

My cousin Debra was in school during the week. However, on the weekends when Debra was home, she and I liked to play outside together. Sometimes, Debra would visit her friends on the weekends. Her best friend, Tammy, had a couple of horses, and Debra loved to ride the horses with Tammy. She loved riding so much that she talked Uncle Richard into buying her a horse of her very own. Uncle Richard bought a couple of horses so that he could ride along with Debra. I remember the first time Uncle Richard and Debra went riding. Of course, I wanted to ride with them. I sat on Uncle Richard's horse with him as he and Debra took off.

As we began to ride out of the backyard, the sun was beating down on us, and there were only a few small, scattered clouds in the sky and a gentle breeze to help cool us. As we got closer to the woods, a good distance away from the house, the trees got closer and closer together. The tree tops provided relief for us, blocking the sun's hot rays. We zigzagged through the thick woods on the horses. All of a sudden, we heard the unmistakable sound of drum beats. They were Native American drum beats. We rode a little further, continuing to zigzag until Uncle Richard stopped suddenly, prompting Debra to stop next to us. Uncle Richard pointed to a tree top and said, "Debra, look up there." Both my eyes and Debra's followed the direction Uncle Richard was pointing in. Up in the tree was a black cat. It was lying on its stomach, draped over a pretty thick branch, with its front legs dangling from one side of the branch and its back legs hanging listlessly from the other side. It was obvious that the cat was dead.

The drum beats grew louder and louder. Uncle Richard said, "Let's get back to the house now!" I didn't know at that time, as a child, that there was a Native American cemetery back in the woods where we rode that day. Uncle Richard and Debra discovered it the second time they rode their horses, and from that day on, they always rode in the opposite direction of the cemetery.

Uncle Richard taught me a lot of things while Mother and I lived with them. There were so many good and interesting times at Uncle Richard and Aunt Sue's house. Eventually, the time came when my mother could finally afford a home of her own. She had found a decent paying job — at least one that would pay the rent — and she wanted to move back to Texas. She also wanted to venture out on her own and grow a family with Berry and me.

CHAPTER TWO

Our Party of Five

Mother found a small apartment for us to live in. It was nothing fancy, but it was a roof over our heads, and it was a home of our very own. Berry came home whenever he could take leave. Each time, Mother and I would pick him up at the airport. I would stand by my mother's side, and we would wait anxiously for Berry. I remember watching him walk toward us in his green army uniform, and when he would finally reach us, he would hug and kiss Mother, and then bend over and pick me up, covering my cheeks with kisses.

We were a happy little family, or so that is what we appeared to be to me and to the strangers around us. But our close family members and friends were not so convinced. They knew different. They saw the bruises on

Mom that she tried to cover with makeup but couldn't because the bruises were just too big, black, and purple. Mother still loved Berry regardless. He would always sweet-talk her. He used the language that I realized later in life is the language that abusers use: "I'm so sorry;" "That's not who I really am;" "I can't believe I did that;" "It won't ever happen again;" and, "Things are going to change and be better, I promise." He would apologize to Mother after each time he hit her. She would always forgive him, so he kept coming home to us on leave.

And then one day, all of a sudden, I had a little baby sister, Kristine. Mother told me that the Easter Bunny had brought her. Kristine was born on April 6, which that year happened to be Easter Sunday. I think I told Mother to tell the Easter Bunny to take her back. I also remember thinking that Kristine looked like Bugs Bunny, because she had the roundest, puffiest little cheeks. In time, I was so very happy that the Easter Bunny hadn't taken her back because I realized that I loved her, and I decided to call her Sissy.

Another couple of years passed by, and along came baby sister Carrie. Not long after Carrie was born, I saw my stepfather hit my mother for the very first time. My aunt Cassie, who is 10 years older than I am, was visiting — thank God. I remember my stepfather was talking, being mean to my mother. My mother picked up Carrie and walked into the bathroom. My stepfather followed them. He reached for the towel rack that was attached to the wall. He put his hand around it and jerked it off the wall. He aimed for my mother's head and swung, hitting her in the forehead. She fell backward, unconscious, into the bathtub, never letting go of Carrie. I was only four years old when this happened, and with my little eyes I watched my mother get struck in the head with the towel rack and then fall backward into the tub.

Mother and Carrie did not make a move or a sound. My aunt Cassie was crying. She picked up Kristine, who was playing on the living room floor with her Raggedy Ann doll and then walked over to me. I stood frozen by the bathroom door, looking at my mother and baby sister lying in the tub. Berry was still standing by the tub. Aunt Cassie, with Kristine on her hip, took my hand and hurried to the hall closet. She sat us both down inside it and told us to stay there and be quiet until she came back to get us. She closed the door, and a dark silence engulfed Sissy and me. We waited. The only sounds were the pulse of my heartbeat drumming like a tiny hammer in my chest and Kristine's rapid breathing.

After what seemed like an eternity, Sissy started crying and, being the big sister, I wanted to comfort her and take care of her. I hugged her and told her, "Sissy, it's going to be okay. Shush. Don't cry. We have to be quiet." I then put my little arms around her in the pitch-dark closet, and I hugged her tight.

My aunt Cassie came back and opened the closet door. She said, "It's all okay now."

Aunt Cassie had called my grandmother, and a few minutes after we had been let out of the closet, my grandmother, "Mama Carson," arrived and wanted to know where Berry was. I didn't know it at the time, but Mama Carson had her shotgun with her in the back seat of her car. Thank goodness Berry had left or else he would have been in big trouble with my grandmother. My mother regained consciousness, and my baby sister Carrie was untouched and unharmed. I remember thinking, why would my daddy do such a horrible, ugly thing to my mommy and little sister?

I was told of only one prior beating before this one. It was before my baby sister Carrie was born. Mother and Berry had dropped Sissy and me off at Mama Carson's house so that Aunt Cassie could watch over us while Mother and Berry went to a friend's party. When they arrived at the party, mother sat down on the couch while Berry walked into the kitchen to get a beer. While mother was sitting on the couch, a young man approached and talked to her briefly. Berry walked out of the kitchen and stood a short distance across the living room. He saw the young man talking to Mother. Mother told the young man that she was at the party with her husband, and the young man walked away. Berry walked over to mother and said to her, "You think you are so beautiful, don't you?"

Mother looked at Berry and replied, "No," but Berry met her response by giving her an ugly look and hitting her in the face with the glass beer bottle he was holding. It struck her just above her nose, and the bottle shattered into pieces. Mother's forehead was cut wide open, and blood started to gush out. The blood dripped all over her clothes and onto the living room floor. There was a lot of blood everywhere. Some of Mother's friends at the party heard the loud noise and turned to see Mother covered in blood. Shocked by what they saw, they quickly ran to her side and began putting pressure on the cuts while helping her to someone's car and rushing her to the hospital. At the hospital, Mother got stitches across her lower forehead. She did not press any charges against Berry.

The next morning, Mother woke us up, even though she was clearly in so much pain from her injury. Mother never did and still never does miss a beat being our mother, no matter what. Sissy and I looked at Mother and didn't recognize her. Who was this scary looking monster who has our mother's voice? We immediately started crying and tried to get away from her. "It's okay," she said. "It's mommy, babies." We didn't believe her; we were confused and scared. She sounded like Mommy, but it couldn't be her because this was a very scary looking monster. Mother's face and both of her eyes were swollen. Her eyes were black, blue, and purple. We could see the stitches on her face. She was completely unrecognizable to us. Mother started crying also. She realized that she was unrecognizable to us and that it was terrifying us. She called Mama Carson to come pick Sissy and me up. Mama Carson and Aunt Cassie watched over us until mother's face healed.

My stepfather not only hit and beat my mother, but he also started staying away from home for longer periods of time. My mother said to us when we got a little older that he had run into some trouble while he was on base and that he was staying there for a little while longer. And the truth of the matter was that he was spending most of his time in the stockade because he was drinking and starting fights with the other soldiers on base. It was both a blessing and a curse for my mother. On the one hand, he was not at home to beat her; however, on the other hand, Mother knew that when he got out and returned home that he was going to get drunk and then come home and beat her up.

Berry had been away for a while, and I guess he wanted to make a good impression on my mother again — like he had tried to do so many times before but had failed over and over — because he showed up one Easter Sunday to take me and Sissy somewhere and in his arms were two big, stuffed rabbits. One was purple and one pink, and he said I could choose mine first because I was the oldest. I chose the purple one. My mother always had faith in him, and she loved Berry, despite him beating her. She wanted to believe that this time he meant what he said when he told her that he was sorry and that he would be a much better husband and father. So away we went.

He put us in the back seat of his car, and we drove off, waving bye to Mother through the back window while standing up in the back seat. I do not know exactly where we went that day, only that he stopped and parked on the side of a big bridge. An embankment covered with large white rocks led straight down to an expansive lake. He got out of the car, opened the back door, and let us out. I stood there next to Berry, looking at the water. It was windy. The waves in the lake had white caps on them, and the wind sent the waves crashing into the white rocks. I then noticed that Sissy had taken off climbing down the rocks. She was headed straight for the water. Berry stood there silent and motionless; he was just watching her as she crawled closer and closer to the water. I realized that he was not going after her to keep her from getting into the big lake, so I yelled her name and started climbing down the rocks after her. I caught up to her pretty quickly and grabbed her little hand, telling her that we needed to go back up now. As we started the long climb back up the big white rocks, I looked up at Berry, who was still just standing there looking down at us, not moving an inch or saying anything — just looking at us. I remember thinking that it was so hard, trying to climb back up all the big white rocks with Sissy. Berry, as we drew closer and closer to him, still did and said absolutely nothing to help me get her up to the very top of the embankment. Finally, we reached the top and headed toward the bridge, where Berry still stood with a trance-like stare in his eyes. He suddenly snapped out of it, looked down at us, and turned toward the car. He started walking over to it. We followed behind him, and I was not letting go of Sissy's little hand. Berry opened the back door of the car. I walked Sissy over to the back of the car where Berry stood with his hand on the door, waiting for us to climb in. We climbed into the car. Berry got into the front, and we were off again, headed somewhere else.

Sitting in the back seat, still clutching Sissy's little hand, I remember thinking how happy I was to have my Sissy safe in the car with me. The next stop we made was at a woman's house. A woman who I had never seen before. We all got out of the car and walked up to her front door. Berry knocked on the door; she opened it. We all three walked in. The woman walked over to some toys that she had in the corner of her living room. She picked them up and carried them to the coffee table centered between her couch and loveseat. Berry told Sissy and me to sit down on the floor next to the woman's coffee table. The woman said, "There you go." Berry told Sissy and me to play with the toys and to stay there. He then walked into another room with the dark-haired woman and closed the door behind them. I looked around the living room as I wondered what we were doing and why we were there.

Sissy played with the toys. A little while later Berry and the woman came out. Berry looked at her and said, "I will talk to you later," and then we left the woman's house.

I was so happy to return home to Mother. What an exhausting day for a little girl, who had watched over her little sister and kept her from danger. As a child, I had no idea what was going on at the time, on that day. It was not until later, when I was old enough to look back, that I knew exactly what had happened. Berry was in that woman's bedroom with her, and they were not in there just whistling Dixie. I have no explanation for the bridge incident; I only remember it. And I cannot come up with any excuse for a father who allows his two very young daughters — just two and four years old — to go down a steep bridge side, with huge rocks leading to a big lake, by themselves, without intervening. There is no excuse for that.

My mother had to work two jobs just to make ends meet with Berry enlisted in the army and with him spending most of his time locked up in the stockade. He was not sending any money home to help her pay the bills. Every morning mother got up and went to work. She did not return home until after we had already been put in bed and we were fast asleep. My aunt Cassie watched over us. There was hardly any food in the house.

One Wednesday, Aunt Cassie went into the kitchen to make us some lunch. She looked in all the cabinets and then the icebox. There was nothing. The cabinets were bare, and the icebox had just one stick of butter and a pitcher of tea. She had emptied the last of the cereal into our breakfast bowls and had poured the last of the milk over it. She had skipped breakfast herself and was also hungry. She walked into the living room and picked up her purse. She took out her coin pouch. She had just enough money for a loaf of bread and a gallon of milk, but not enough for lunchmeat. She had to feed us lunch. She walked us over to the grocery store that was just behind where we lived. We walked in and headed down the lunchmeat aisle. She looked all around her. She quickly stuck a package of lunchmeat inside her blue jeans and pulled her shirt over loosely so that the small bulge was not evident. We then proceeded to the bread aisle. She picked up a loaf of bread. Then we walked to the milk section, and she picked up a gallon of milk. As we walked to the checkout, I was hoping and praying that no one had seen her put the lunchmeat inside her pants. Aunt Cassie put the milk and bread on the checkout counter. Aunt Cassie seemed calm, but my heart was racing. I knew that it was wrong to steal. The woman working the register looked at her. She smiled and asked, "How are you doing?" as she picked up the bread and milk and entered the amounts of each.

"I'm good. How are you?" Aunt Cassie replied.

"I can't complain," the woman said. "Your total is one dollar and fifty cents."

Aunt Cassie pulled the money out of her little coin pouch and handed it to the woman. The woman put the milk and bread in a brown paper sack and then handed it to Cassie with a pleasant, "Have a nice day."

We walked out of the store as fast as we could. My heart was still pounding. "Come on, babies," Aunt Cassie said. "Let's go eat some lunch."

Aunt Cassie had never stolen anything before, nor did she ever again that I know of, but on that day she did. There was no food in the house, and she did not have the money to buy the lunchmeat. Aunt Cassie needed money and a real paying job. Mother could not afford to pay her much for watching over us. Aunt Cassie found a job in the employment section of the newspaper. That meant that she could no longer watch over us while Mother was at work all day and night. My mother had a friend at work who told her about a woman who loved children and who was a Christian. My mother was so lucky to have found such a nice woman — Mrs. Henderson. Mrs. Henderson knew Mother could only afford to pay her very little or nothing, like she had paid Aunt Cassie. But Mrs. Henderson did not care. She was indeed a Christian, and she had also been a single mother herself. She had raised two boys of her own. She wanted to help Mother out and she did just that.

She watched over us pretty much all day and night. I remember Mrs. Henderson would feed us meals and then also give us snacks. She tucked us in at night, and we said our prayers just before she turned out the lights. We would fall asleep and wake up to our mother's soft voice, saying, "Wake up, sweetheart. It's time to go." She would come to pick us up late at night. We were so sleepy-eyed that she had to pick us up out of bed and carry us out to the car. The very next day, it was the same thing all over again.

I don't know how my mother did all this by herself — working two jobs and taking care of small children. In my eyes, she is today and was back then Wonder Woman, my hero. She could have easily said to heck with it all and given up, but she didn't. She worked very hard day and night just to put a roof over our heads. All this despite being married to an abusive man who drank all the time and became violent, and who never provided her with any real financial support at all. We lived in several different houses in McKinney when I was very young, and it's a sad thing that my stepfather did not help pay the rent. I guess as a young child, I somehow noticed that fact. So, when my stepfather showed up one day in his brand new pickup truck, I got in it and bit the dashboard as hard as I could with my little teeth, leaving indentations that would remain forever. Both my mother and he asked me, "Why did you do that?"

"Because I wanted to," I replied.

The days continued to pass, and I got older and older. It was time for me to start school. My mother did not want to send me to kindergarten, so I skipped it and started first grade at Prosper Elementary School in Prosper, Texas, which was a town right next to McKinney, at the age of six. I remember my first grade teacher's name was Mrs. Forest. She was a very nice woman. She had short, dark brown hair. She was very pretty. Every day in class she would ask, "Who wants to learn their ABCs today and who wants to color?"

I would always say that I wanted to color. Eventually, all my other classmates had agreed to learn their ABCs, one or two of them each day, until they were all seated on the big round rug on the other side of the classroom. I was seated at a little table by myself coloring when Mrs. Forest said to me, "Julie, it's time to learn your ABCs now."

I looked at her and replied, "I am happy with just coloring; I don't need to learn my ABCs because I color so pretty." I held up the picture that I had been coloring and gave her a big smile.

She smiled back at me and said simply, "How lovely." To make a long story short, I ended up learning my ABCs. I also learned how to read. I liked books. My favorite book was *The Little Red Hen*.

While in first grade, I rode the bus back and forth to school. The home we moved into and lived in when I started first grade was a single-wide trailer. When it was cold outside, my mother would wake me up to get me ready for school. I would sit up, slip my little feet into my house shoes, and walk into the kitchen, where my mother had the oven turned on low with the oven door open and two chairs sitting right in front of it. The low oven temperature was just enough heat to warm me as my mother would help me get dressed and ready for school. I would even eat my breakfast while sitting in the chair in front of the oven.

Living there, I experienced a couple of amazing things. One day while I was outside playing, I found a caterpillar with black and yellow stripes. I picked it up and took it into the house to show my mother. She went into her bedroom, got a shoebox, and put the caterpillar in it for me.

The next thing I knew, the caterpillar was missing! It was not in the box anymore. We looked everywhere for it, and we had almost given up until my mother said, "Julie, look up there," as she pointed up with her finger. Up high on the tall living room curtains, in the very top corner of them, there it was, but it looked different. My mother explained to me that it was sleeping, and when it wakes up, it will come out of its cocoon as a butterfly. Boom! That blew my mind, and I wondered how on earth that was possible. I was so excited and could not wait to see the beautiful butterfly that would come out of the cocoon.

Days passed, and sure enough, there it was: a beautiful monarch butterfly. Its tiny, thin black legs were holding onto the opened cocoon. Its beautiful orange and brown wings were opening and closing gently and repeatedly. Mother told me that it was drying its wings so it could take flight. I thought, wow, it's beautiful, but how were we going to keep this beautiful butterfly in the house? What should I feed it? As all these questions ran through my little mind, my mother started explaining to me that I could not keep it anymore. She said we had to let it fly free outside. I was so sad, but I knew that my mother was smart and that I had to let the butterfly go free. Mother caught the butterfly with her hands, cupping them gently around it so that she would not rub off any of the powder on the butterfly's wings. She asked me to open the front door, and once we were outside, she opened up her hands and let it go. It flew away free.

I loved playing outside in the front yard. I had an all-blue plastic Bambi deer. It was the perfect size to hold in my small hand. It was indeed my favorite toy of the few toys that I had. I loved playing with it. I pressed its little hooves into the dirt and made little deer tracks. Our summers were hot, but in the front yard, right up against our trailer home, there was shade, and it provided some relief from the summer sun when I was playing outside.

My mother always dressed me appropriately for the weather. There was a woman in our trailer park who my mother had met. The woman sewed clothes. She had made me a couple of little romper outfits. My favorite one was yellow with pink flowers all over it. One day while I was playing outside and wearing it, I walked over to the creek that ran beside the trailer park. I looked at the water in the creek and then I looked up. My little eyes saw a bald eagle flying overhead. Its wings were spread out full and straight as it glided while it looked down at the water. It was a huge bird. It was the most beautiful bird I had ever seen.

Living in the neighborhood, we had met several neighbors. The neighbor right next to us had a couple of older daughters who had a couple of horses — a mama horse and a baby horse. One weekend afternoon, the oldest daughter asked me if I could help her with the horses. Of course, I said yes! She asked me to come stand on their back porch and hold a halter lead rope that was attached to the baby horse. She then took the mama horse around to the front of the house, leaving me alone with the baby horse, which suddenly started to act a little crazy. It was jumping back and forth, rearing up, trying to pull away from me. Boy howdy did that make me all jumpy too. I let go of that lead rope real fast and I said, "Go if you want to go." And it sure did. It took right off running.

The girl came back and asked, "Where is the baby horse?"

"I don't know where it's at," I confessed. I felt really bad.

The girl ended up catching the baby horse. She never asked me to hold onto a lead rope for their horses again. That was okay with me, because I didn't like being in that situation. That baby horse wasn't really much of a baby to me anyway. It was really big, and it scared me when it started jumping around and acting crazy.

Also while living there, during my first grade year of school, Berry had straightened up some. He was around us more, and he was actually trying to be a decent man — a decent father. Well, the best he knew how to be.

CHAPTER THREE

The Little White Tin House

By the time I had finished first grade in Prosper, Berry had also finished his service in the army. He took over and started running his father, Gerald's, air conditioning and heating business. We moved to a town called Melissa. My mother and stepfather purchased some land and had a brick house built on it. It had three bedrooms, two full bathrooms, a kitchen, and a living room. We lived there for a couple of years, but Mom and Berry couldn't make the payments on the house any longer, so Gerald and his wife, Barbara, bought it. We moved back to McKinney into a house.

A month later, a little white tin house that sat right next to the brick house that my mother and stepfather had built a couple of years earlier came up for sale, and Gerald told

Berry about it. My mother and Berry moved quickly and purchased the little white tin house. It was a very cheap price for the house and land. We moved into it. The house was wrapped all the way around in wavy, white, corrugated tin, like the kind used to build barns and sheds. The roof of the house was also tin, and it was silver. The tin house had two bedrooms, one bathroom, a living room, a kitchen, and a dining room, with a pretty good-sized storage closet in the dining room. Mother filled the house with her old furniture. It was an old house, with old flooring and old fixtures. It had old everything inside and out. But as soon as we moved in, my mother began cleaning it. She scrubbed and scrubbed, until it was an old shiny house, all cleaned up. The house sat on one acre of land with a barn and a garage with an attached work shed behind it. It also had a little bonus shed on the side of the garage. I guess it had been built to store a lawnmower in, but my sisters and I had other plans for it: we made it our little playhouse.

There were fourteen pecan trees on the property. Some of them were really tall and big; some were little. There was one big pecan tree in the front yard that Sissy and I started climbing as soon as we moved into the house. Sissy decided to climb it alone one afternoon. I was in the house with Mother and Carrie. Sissy came running into the house and into the kitchen where mother was making dinner, as Carrie and I sat and colored pictures at the dining room table. Sissy was breathing fast. My mother looked at her and said, "What is the matter?"

Sissy was holding her chest. "I fell out of the tree," she uttered.

Mom rushed to her side to examine her. She put her hands on Sissy and began feeling her from head to toes, moving Sissy's long, wavy blonde hair to the side so she could check around Sissy's neck. "Do you hurt anywhere?" Mother asked her.

"No," Sissy said, still gasping for air.

"You're okay," Mom assured her.

"No, I'm not," Sissy countered. "It almost killed me to death."

With that, Mother hugged her tightly and smiled. "Please do not climb the trees anymore. It's dangerous, and I don't want you getting hurt."

After that, we waited a good while before we climbed the trees again. When we got moved in and everything had been put up in the house, my sisters and I explored like we had never explored before. There was so much to discover outside.

Months passed and Christmas arrived before we knew it. We put up our first Christmas tree there in the little white tin house. Berry drove us down the highway. He stopped his truck next to a field that was covered in cedar trees. We all got out of his truck. It was cold outside with gray clouds over us. We walked out into the field. Berry walked with us, carrying his axe. "Which one should we choose?" he asked.

My sisters and I pointed to a big, thick, tall tree. We jumped up and down with excitement and also because the winter wind had picked up and we were shivering. Berry had his eyes on a smaller one, with way fewer branches on it. It was a Charlie Brown Christmas tree if I'd ever seen one. "How about this one?" he asked.

We were cold and not fussy children, so we acquiesced. He chopped down the little Charlie Brown Christmas tree with only a couple of whacks. We loaded it into the back of his truck and took it home. Mother helped us make an old-fashioned paper chain to go around the tree and some ornaments. For the tree topper, we made a beautiful paper star with glitter on it. Even though it was modest in size, it was the most beautiful Christmas tree ever.

My sister Carrie wanted a Davy Crockett gun and hat for Christmas, and by golly, she got them. I have no idea where my mother bought them. Carrie also got a puppy that she named Charlie Brown. Carrie was a tomboy, and she always ran around in just her panties. That Christmas she had also asked for boy underwear, which she also got. When we were young, my mother and Berry could not afford to buy us a lot or anything expensive for Christmas. Mother did her shopping at the Goodwill store. It was not much; it was little or nothing to most people or children; but to us, Mother's gifts were treasures, and we loved everything that she ever bought for us.

I was in second grade at the school in Melissa. My sisters and I rode the bus to school. Of course, there's a bully in every school, and our school was no exception. The bully in our school just happened to live right down the road from us, and his name was Bill. He had a loud, mean mouth. And he made fun of everyone. He made ugly comments about our house. On the way home from school one day, he walked to the back of the bus where my sisters and I sat. He looked at me and said, "You live in a barn." He said this in front of all the other kids on the bus.

"That's mean," I said. "We do not live in a barn; it's a house."

As the bus approached and stopped at the end of our driveway, my sisters and I stood up to get off the bus. Bill started saying over and over, "You live in a barn."

I completely ignored him, as my sisters and I walked past him toward the front of the bus. I figured ignoring him was the best thing to do. Well, that bully just so happened to be my age and in my classroom at school.

Back then, we still took naps every day at our school. One particular day during nap time, Bill scooted his nap mat right up against mine. I was lying on my side, and he was behind me. He put his arm around my waist and hugged me, as he inched closer to me until he was right up against my backside. I turned around so that I was facing him and pushed him away from me. I turned back around, and he did the same thing again. I also did the very same thing again. I told him to stop it or I will tell the teacher. It was on that day that I realized that he liked me; however, I did not like him.

He did not have very many friends and that was due to him being a bully. He tried many times to get me to be his girlfriend and went a little too far one day on the playground. I was playing tag with my friends. He walked up to me and grabbed me. He put his arms around me, holding me tight. He tried to kiss me. I wiggled and pulled my right arm loose from his grip and punched him right in the eye with all of my might. He let go of me and put his hands over his face. He was in pain. As soon as I was completely free from his strong arms and gross lips, I ran into the school building and hid in a classroom under a desk. As I sat there alone in a vacant classroom, I started to laugh. My heart was racing a million beats a minute, and it felt like my little heart might just beat its way out of my chest. I thought, wow, I got him good! I was scared though. I was scared that he would come looking for me in the school building and try to hit me back, but he never did, and that hard punch I gave him made him scared of me. The very next day, he came to school with a black eye. He never tried anything like that ever again with me.

Our favorite time of the year — well, maybe not my mother's favorite time — was summertime. Summertime meant no school for three full months. During the summer, Mom let us invite our friends and cousins over. We loved to roast weenies and marshmallows by a fire in our backyard. Mother would get everything ready to go ahead of time and would closely supervise us anytime we had a weenie roast. Some of our friends and cousins would stay the night on weenie roast nights. When the summer sun would start to set, we would get excited! My mother would light the wood, sticks, and newspapers that she had gathered. The fire was surrounded by big rocks, and we used wire coat hangers that my mother had unwound as roasting sticks. My mother would put the wieners on the coat hangers, and we would hold them over the fire. Some kids only cooked them a minute and others, like me, burnt them to a crisp. Once the wieners were all consumed it was time for marshmallows — my favorite part. After we had eaten everything, we would sit around the fire and listen to it crackle. We talked and told scary stories. Those were some of the best times ever.

Sissy and I shared a bedroom. Mother had put bunk beds in our room. We took turns sleeping on the top bunk. One school night, mother tucked us into bed and went back to the kitchen where she was making cherry chip cookies — yummy! They were my second favorite, next to chocolate. The smell of the delicious cookies kept me awake, even after she had finished baking and cleaning everything up in the kitchen. She went to bed. I laid there and enjoyed the aroma of the cookies for as long as I could, until my sleepy little eyes gave up and the inevitable happened: they closed. I was sound asleep on the top bunk.

The next thing I remember is being awakened from a dead sleep to the sound of my stepfather's truck barreling up the driveway and coming to a screeching stop. The rocks that covered the driveway were thrown all over the yard, and some even hit our tin house, which made a very loud noise. The next thing I heard was the front door being swung wide open and hitting the wall behind it. Then I could hear objects being knocked over and broken inside the house. I knew that my stepfather was drunk, and I knew that he was going to go into my mother's bedroom and start hitting her. My feet hit the floor just like that, and so did Sissy's. We held hands as we unlocked the back door. We left the back door open. We ran as fast as we could around the side of the house and straight into the cornfield. The corn stalks were very tall, so they hid us. We sat together, holding hands, as we cried. We could hear banging and loud noises coming from the house, along with screaming. We shook with fear and terror, as we could do nothing because we were only little girls. We waited for the beating of my mother to stop, while we sat down on the dirt, in our little nightgowns, barefoot, in the cornfield.

My little sister Carrie had stayed by our mother's side the whole time Berry was beating on our mother. Carrie hit my stepfather. She had jumped onto his back and was hitting him on his back, as he had knocked Mother down onto the floor and was on top of her, hitting her with his fist.

Berry was so drunk he finally stopped hitting our mom. Mother got up off the floor in pain. Her face and chest hurt from the punches. She saw that the back door had been opened and realized that Sissy and I were outside. She walked out holding Carrie's hand, calling out for me and Sissy. Still sitting in the cornfield, we stood up to the sound of her voice calling out. We were crying, inching our way slowly toward the direction of her voice. As we got close to her, we peeked through the corn stalks to make sure my stepfather was not there anywhere. We crossed the barbed wire fence the same way we had on our way into the cornfield: carefully, but we were less fearful coming out of the cornfield than we had been going in because we knew that if we didn't see my stepfather outside, then he was passed out and asleep inside the house. We knew then that he was no longer going to terrorize us and beat our mother up that night. Our mother walked us back into the house and tucked us back into bed. We woke up the next morning and went to school. My stepfather's drinking became a weekly thing. At least once a week and most times twice a week, he came home drunk, and we knew what that meant, what that always led to: the beating of our poor mother.

Berry was not the only thing that scared us. There was something else. We could not see it, but we definitely heard it. One afternoon after school, before my mother got home, Kristine, Carrie, and I were playing tag inside the house. We probably should not have been, and if mother had been there, we would not have been. Mother let us stay by ourselves just for an hour after school. She did not have anyone to watch us or the money to pay anyone to watch us, so we stayed by ourselves. I had been tagged "it," and I quickly went for Carrie, as she could not run as fast as Kristine. I reached out for Carrie and tagged her. She surprised me and came quickly at me in the kitchen. I started running into the bedroom that I shared with Kristine. I had just made it past our bedroom door when it somehow slammed shut on Carrie's fingers as she reached out to tag me. She started screaming and crying, as did Kristine, who was standing on the other side of the door with Carrie. "Open the door!" Kristine yelled.

I turned around and tried to open it. But it wouldn't budge. I tried to pull and jiggle the knob. I even pleaded with God for help. After a couple of minutes of us screaming and crying, it suddenly opened. Carrie held her fingers. They were very red. I told them over and over again that I was not the one who had shut the door; I did not touch it. Kristine had been standing behind Carrie when the door had shut, and she had seen it slam shut all by itself. At the time, we did not think too hard about who, what, or why the door had slammed shut. We were only focused on Carrie and her fingers. I told Carrie to go to the bathroom.

I followed her into it. I told her to put her hand under the faucet, and I ran cold water over it as she continued to cry. Mother had some medicine and bandages in the bathroom closet. I wrapped some bandages around Carrie's fingers. There was no blood, but they were all scratched up and red in color.

Mother came home several minutes later. We told her what had happened. She took the bandages off of Carrie's fingers to inspect the damage. She asked Carrie to move her fingers, and she slowly moved each of them. "Why were y'all running in the house? You know you cannot do that; you will get hurt."

We promised Mom that we would not run in the house again. And we kept our promise to her. We were so happy that Carrie's fingers were not broken. Several days passed with no doors slamming shut again, but that wasn't the end of frightening experiences that our young minds couldn't explain.

One night I was lying in bed on the bottom bunk, still awake about thirty minutes after Mom had bathed us, combed our long blonde hair, and tucked us into our beds. All the lights were turned off, but I couldn't fall asleep. Our room was lit by the moonlight coming through the sheer curtains that Mother had hung when we first moved in. Our bedroom door was open, and I heard someone walking around in the kitchen. Our old wood floors creaked with each step anyone ever took on them. The walking, creaking sound got close to our bedroom door. I looked over to the open door, expecting to see my mother standing there. No. It wasn't her; it wasn't anyone in fact.

How could that be? Someone had to be there. I could still hear the creaking of the wood floor, and before I knew it, the footsteps made their way into our bedroom. I was thinking, who is this person, that I cannot see, but can hear walking? The footsteps walked to the center of our bedroom and then began to walk in a circle. I was absolutely terrified. I pulled my covers up over my head. The creaking footsteps continued to walk in a circle, making two complete circles in the center of our room before leaving and heading back to the kitchen, where they stopped. I slept with the covers over my head that night. I never told Mother about it. This was the second time that the ghost made its presence known to us. And from there on, it was either the ghost or Berry who was frightening us.

CHAPTER FOUR

If Our Walls Could Talk

One of the most terrifying nights I remember was when Berry came into the room I shared with Sissy. He woke us up, pulling the covers off of us as he said, "Get up! I want you to come watch me blow you mother's head off!" He put his hands on us and shook us. We laid in bed too scared to move. He was drunk. "Wake up and come in here! I want y'all to watch me blow your mother's head off," he repeated.

We started shaking and trembling with fright and fear. We started crying; we were terrified. We got out of our small beds and stood up. He walked us into the living room where my mother was sitting in a corner chair. She had been beaten by him; I guess we had been so tired that the sounds of him beating her hadn't woken us this time.

She was sitting in the chair with a chicken leg stuck in her mouth. He lined us girls up in a straight line in front of my mother. He then walked over to his shotgun that was leaning against the wall. He picked up his shotgun and stood to the side of us and pointed the shotgun at my mother's head, looking directly at her. My sisters and I stood shaking uncontrollably and crying in our bare feet and our little nightgowns. I wanted to run and try to get help, but I could not move. I was frozen in fear. I thought quickly to myself that if I tried to run to get help, he would shoot me. I thought, if I run and leave, he will shoot my mother and sisters too. So, I quickly decided that I should stay there with my sisters and mother. Our only hope was to beg and plead with him. "Please, please don't shoot our mommy," we cried.

Berry appeared to be listening to what we were saying, and he looked away from our mother and over at us. But his face revealed nothing but pure evil, and a laugh escaped from his twisted mouth. He looked back at our mother and moved his finger around the trigger, pretending to pull it. He laughed a wicked laugh and said, "Boom! Boom!"

My sisters and I were crying and screaming. We thought our mother was going to die. Then, inexplicably, a calm feeling came over me. I believed God was watching over us. I believed he had sent angels down immediately to protect us all. Berry did not pull the trigger. The evil laugh and look he had had stopped all of a sudden. He lowered the shotgun and walked into his and mother's bedroom.

My mother got up out of the chair. She walked us back into our bedroom and tucked us back into bed. "It's over now. It's okay, sweethearts. Go to sleep."

The next morning, my mother woke us up to get us ready for school just like normal while Berry slept. We walked to the end of our long driveway and waited for the bus. I was so scared to leave the house. I was hoping and praying that Berry would not hurt my mother. The bus stopped at the end of the driveway and the door opened. My sisters and I climbed up the steps, and the bus driver closed the door behind us. I sat down in a seat next to my sisters. I looked out the bus window at our house. I felt sick to my stomach. There was a fear in the pit of my stomach that Berry would hurt mom too badly or possibly even kill her. My head bobbed backward as the bus driver drove forward down the road in front of our house. My eyes stayed fixated on our little tin house until I could no longer see it.

We arrived at school and walked into the building. We pretended that everything was okay. And we went from classroom to classroom, talking to our friends throughout the day, all the while our little hearts, bodies, minds, and souls kept hoping and wishing for a normal, happy, family life at home — a normal and happy life like our friends talked about, like we had experienced while visiting and staying the night at their houses.

Our home life was anything but normal and happy. My sisters and I were living in hell. And yet, somehow, we managed to carry on as if nothing was going on, as if it was all normal and happy at home for us too. There were moments of normalcy, at least for a few hours, when we would go to family gatherings for holidays. We visited with our many cousins, aunts, uncles, and, of course, our grandmother Mama Carson, who at Thanksgiving made some very yummy food and desserts. After eating, all the children would go out in her big yard to play together. And at Christmas time, we had yummy food and desserts again, but once all the plates were clean the children would be anxious to open gifts. Mama Carson had had eight children, but the eighth was a stillborn boy. Mama Carson had buried him in a tiny coffin. She had been heartbroken and devastated. Her seven surviving children — my four aunts and three uncles — had all had children of their own, except for my youngest aunt and uncle, who never married or had children. Our lives were somewhat normal during these holiday get-togethers. But if Berry drank while we were there, he would start yelling and slapping my mother as soon as we got into the car. We girls would sit in the back seat crying, scared and helpless.

We also went to Berry's family's holiday gatherings. We had fun there sometimes when we played a game with the children and adults together. It was called "spoons." We would sit in a circle with spoons in the middle — one less spoon than we had people. Then we'd each get four playing cards. We'd take turns drawing a card from the deck and then passing a card to the person on the left. The idea was to get four of a kind and grab a spoon as quickly as possible. Once anyone grabbed a spoon, everyone else had to grab one too. The person left with no spoon was out. We would also try to fake people out and pretend to grab a spoon because if someone grabbed a spoon when another person was faking, he or she would be out.

All of Berry's family thought that Mother and us girls were not good enough to be in the family. Berry's mother, Anna, told all of her friends that I was not her granddaughter, and Berry's three sisters had nothing to do with us, except during holiday gatherings when they pretended to be aunts. Our cousins, however, liked us and we had lots of fun with them. Berry would always drink on the holidays there.

After leaving a Christmas Eve gathering there one year, Berry started arguing with Mother during the drive home. He punched her hard in the side of her head. I was holding my Cher doll that I had gotten as a gift. I let go of it and dropped it. Berry pulled the car over onto the shoulder of the major highway we were on and started punching her over and over. Carrie was screaming for Berry to stop from the back seat directly behind him. Sissy was seated in the middle. I opened the back car door and got out, leaving the door open. Sissy climbed out of the back seat, and we started running toward a nearby exit ramp together. I didn't know where we were going to run to exactly; I only knew that I wanted to run away from Berry beating my mother.

Mother opened her car door and yelled out to us to come back. We stopped and turned around but yelled, "No!" We were scared and crying.

She got out of the car and demanded that we come back. We walked back to the car and got in. Mother closed the back door after we climbed into the back seat. We were right back where we'd started.

"Where in the hell do y'all think y'all were going?" Berry asked.

Crying and shaking, I said to him, "We were scared. We don't like it when you hit mom."

"You can't run down a highway in the middle of the night," he said, starting up the car and pulling back onto the highway.

Except for the sniffles coming from the back seat, silence filled the car all the way home. When we got home, Berry walked straight into the master bedroom, closed the door behind him, and went to sleep.

Berry did try a few times to be a good husband and father. And those times were when he was not drinking. One Christmas, mother got him an electronic, digital chess game. He loved it. He knew how to play chess, and he taught me how to play.

And on Sundays when he wasn't hungover from drinking Saturday night, he would take my sisters and me to do fun things like fishing or riding horses at the stables. Once he even took us to an air show and took us to the local airport to ride in an old biplane — the kind of plane that Snoopy fought the Red Baron in, with two wings and two seats and an open cockpit. When we arrived at the airport that day, Sissy and I were so excited. We were the only two girls who were going to fly that day. Mother and Carrie were with Berry, Sissy, and me. We walked over to the pilot who was going to fly us. Berry shook his hand. The pilot looked at Sissy and me and asked us if we were ready to fly. After our chorus of yeses, he said, "Okay, let me go get the plane ready."

He walked away from us and headed toward a yellow biplane with a target dot painted on the side of it. The pilot waved us over. Another man was waiting by the airplane hangar, and he got into an old red pickup truck and

Chapter Four: *If Our Walls Could Talk*

drove it over to the biplane and parked it right in front of it. He got out and walked to the back of the truck and pulled out some jumper cables. He attached them to his truck and then to the airplane. He then got back into his truck and cranked it up. The pilot climbed into the back cockpit of the plane and tried to start it up.

"Are they actually trying to jumpstart the airplane?" Mother wondered out loud. "Is that safe?"

"Yeah, they know what they're doing," was Berry's response.

After several attempts, the pilot finally got the plane to start up. He got out of the plane and walked back over to us. "Which one is going first?" he asked, looking at Sissy and me.

"Me!" I shouted.

As the pilot and I walked to the plane, I told him that I wanted to fly low to the ground and that I just wanted to fly in a straight line. I said this to him because Kristine, on the way there earlier, kept saying that she wanted the pilot to do loop tricks with her. I wanted to make sure that I let the pilot know right away, no tricks for me.

"Okay. We can do that," he assured me.

We approached and made it to the plane. The pilot handed me a pair of big goggles. I looked at him with confusion. "You need to wear these to protect your eyes," he explained. "Do you need help putting them on?"

I told him that I did, and he helped me with the goggles. He also helped me into the plane. As I sat down in the front cockpit, he buckled me into the seat. He then got into the cockpit behind me.

"Are you ready for takeoff?" he asked.

"Yes," I said, and the plane started to move. I felt nervous and excited at the same time. We pulled onto the runway and slowly started moving down it, gradually picking up speed until we were moving really fast. The plane lifted up off the pavement. We were airborne. I thought, this is amazing! This is so much fun! We circled around the airport and then headed north. The pilot turned the plane around at the edge of town, and we headed back to the airport. On the way back, I was looking down at the cars, streets, houses, trees, and people we were flying over. I saw our little white tin house and said, "WOW!" It looked so different from that view up in the sky.

We approached the airport, and the pilot lowered the plane and lined it up with the runway. We descended until the wheels of the plane made contact with the pavement. We got out of the plane and walked over to Berry, Mom, Sissy, and Carrie. Berry said to the pilot as he pointed to Sissy, "She wants to do a few loops and a trick or two."

"Okay, you got it," the pilot said, looking at Sissy. They walked over to the biplane, and he helped Sissy with her goggles and helped her into the plane. They pulled onto the runway and soon they were airborne.

The pilot stayed just over the airport as he started doing a big loop in the sky overhead. I could tell my mother was very scared and nervous as she picked up Carrie. The pilot made another big loop and then flew low by the runway, straight across, right in front of us. I looked at my Sissy.

She had those big goggles on, and I thought she looked kinda sick. The pilot then flew the plane straight up into the sky, leveled it out, and then killed the engine. The plane went into a nosedive. It was spiraling around and around. The pilot tried to crank the plane engine up. It did not start. He tried again and again. Still nothing. The plane was getting closer and closer to the pavement. My mother erupted in screams and put Carrie down before running in the direction of the plane. The pilot tried again and again to get the plane started. It would not start. I was getting scared and panicked. I started to cry. Then, miraculously, the engine on the plane started up, just in the nick of time.

Mother was halfway to the plane when she stopped, as the pilot cranked up the engine and leveled the plane out straight. Mother turned around and walked back to us holding her hand over her chest. "I can't believe he killed the engine," she said with disbelief. "They had to jump-start it to begin with."

The pilot landed the plane. He and Sissy got out and walked over to us. Mom walked over to Sissy and picked her up and hugged her tight. The pilot apologized to my mother and Berry. "We ran into a bit of a scare," he said.

I was so glad to see my Sissy safe and okay. I walked over to her, while mother held her. I looked up at her and asked, "Are you okay? Did you get sick doing the loops and trick?"

Sissy looked a bit queasy, and she replied with a shaky, "No, that was fun." But I knew different. I knew she was scared and sick to her stomach after the loops and the nosedive. Needless to say, we never went back to that airport, and we never flew on any of those planes again.

CHAPTER FIVE

A Sliver of Hope

My step-grandfather, Gerald, and his wife, Barbara, who lived right next door to our little white tin house, also drank alcohol. Gerald and Barbara had two kids — a girl Lauren and a boy Mitchel. Lauren and Mitchel were much older than us. Gerald was and had been an abusive man also. He did some pretty mean and scary things too and was mean to Berry and had been mean to Berry the whole time he was growing up. I'm sure that is why Berry was the way he was. But it did not excuse Berry and his behavior. He could have chosen to be different; he could have taken a different path.

One of the craziest things Gerald ever did was show up in our yard in his underwear. My sisters and I were playing in our backyard one afternoon, and Gerald walked up to us wearing nothing but his white underwear and a white towel wrapped around his head. It was obvious he was drunk. Sissy and I looked at each other and started to laugh. "Do y'all want to play?" Gerald asked. "I am the Queen of Sheba."

Sissy and I looked away from him and back at each other and then back to him. We did not know what to think or say. I looked at Gerald, who was standing in front of us, wobbling, swaying back and forth, almost completely naked, and said, "No, we have to go back inside now."

Sissy and I took off running as fast as we could to the house. We went into the house through the back door. We walked over to a window on the back of the house and watched him stumble back to his house. And we couldn't help but laugh.

One weekend during the summer, we went to the lake with Gerald, Barbara, and their two kids. It was hot and sunny. The lake had a sandy beach. We picked out a spot on the beach. I liked the feeling of my feet in the sand. My mother had packed some drinks and food in a Styrofoam cooler. Berry carried it and sat it down on the spot they picked out. Lauren and Mitchel immediately ran and jumped into the water and got wet. I asked mother if I could go into the water, but she told me that I needed to eat first and then she would take us into the water. My sisters and I did not know how to swim. Neither did my mother, but she planned to take us into the shallow water only.

Mother opened up the cooler and gave us our lunches to eat, along with drinks. Barbara yelled to Lauren and

Mitchel to come out of the water to eat. Everyone finished their lunch. My sisters and I played with my mother in the sand. Lauren got out of the water and walked over to Mother and asked her, "Is it okay if I take the girls out into the water, one at a time? I won't take them into the deep water."

"I guess that would be okay as long as you stay in shallow water," Mom told her.

Lauren took Kristine out first. Lauren was holding her in the water and kept going out a little deeper into the water with Sissy as Mom continued to play in the sand with Carrie and me. All of a sudden, Lauren screamed. She was panicked. We looked at her. She was not holding Sissy anymore. Sissy was nowhere in sight.

Lauren was going under water and coming back up. The water was too dark to see through. Lauren continued to go under and then come back up, and each time she resurfaced she had a more panicked look on her face. Mother started screaming. "Help! Someone help!" Mother yelled.

I started crying. I thought, my Sissy is dead; she is gone; I will never see my Sissy again. Lauren went back under one more time, and this time she came back up holding Sissy. Mother grabbed her from Lauren as soon as Lauren reached the beach. Mother held Sissy tight and told us it was time to leave, so we did.

I wondered to myself why Sissy had so many close calls. I thought that maybe I needed to protect her better. Once again, I was so happy and relieved to be home with my Sissy safe with me. The very next summer, Mother enrolled Sissy and me in a summer swim class.

My birthday was fast approaching shortly after the lake scare. And I wanted a pet — a bird to be exact — for my birthday. Mother drove me to the pet store and let me pick out a bird. I picked a blue one and named it Blue Boy. I thought the name was appropriate. I loved him so much. I let him crawl up my arm. He sat on my shoulder. He chirped to me. He was my little friend. Mother had gotten me an antique birdcage. It was black. It also had a tall black stand from which I could hang the birdcage. Every day I would play with my little blue parakeet. I shared him with my sisters so that they could enjoy him too. They also loved him.

One night, Sissy had a bad dream about him. She dreamed that a mouse climbed up the cage stand and onto the birdcage. She dreamed that the mouse opened the birdcage door, climbed inside the birdcage, and grabbed my Blue Boy. She dreamed that the mouse choked my bird until he died. The next morning, Sissy woke up crying. She closed her eyes as she ran past Blue Boy in his birdcage. She told mom about the nightmare she had had. Mother hugged her and told her it was only a bad dream. She showed Sissy that Blue Boy was okay.

The very next morning, when we woke up, Blue Boy was dead. He was lying on the floor right next to the birdcage stand. His neck had been broken. The birdcage door was opened all the way. Did Berry kill my bird while he was drunk? Or was it the ghost in the house with us? I didn't know. Someone or something had killed my bird.

If Berry had killed Blue Boy, it would not have been the first pet he had killed. He had shot and killed Sissy's pet rabbit too. Mother had taken us to the grocery store with her, but before we had left to go to the grocery store, Drew, Berry's best friend, had come over to visit him. Drew had bought a new gun, and he wanted to show it to Berry. Drew had been drinking and had beer in a cooler in the back of his truck. He had given Berry one before Mother said a quick hello to Drew and then put us in the car.

When we returned home that day, Drew's truck was gone, and the trash barrel in the backyard had been lit. Gray smoke rose up from the orange and yellow fire inside the barrel. Berry and Drew had continued to drink after we left, and they had gone out back behind the house to shoot their guns. Berry had decided to use Sissy's rabbit for target practice. He had shot and killed it.

Mother started to put the groceries up, and Sissy and I went outside to play with her rabbit. We looked at the rabbit cage. It was not in there. We ran back into the house to tell Mom that we couldn't find the rabbit; it wasn't in its cage.

Mother walked from the kitchen to the master bedroom and opened the door. Berry was lying on the bed watching TV, drinking. Mother asked him about the rabbit.

He looked at her and laughed. "We shot it."

"Where's the rabbit?" she asked him again.

"I shot it and burned it in the trash barrel."

Mother shook her head back and forth in disbelief and closed the bedroom door. She didn't know that we were standing right behind her until she turned in time to see us start to cry. "I am so sorry babies," she said, hugging us tight.

"Why?" Sissy cried.

"Why did he do that?" I continued.

"I don't know," Mom said. It was clear that she was just as upset as we were. Later that night, Mom tried to explain to Berry that what he had done was horrible, but Berry didn't care. And Mother trying to talk to him only made things worse. Berry kept drinking until he was really drunk. When Mother brought up the rabbit, Berry started hitting her. He screamed at her. Little sister Carrie went into attack mode and tried to pull him away from Mother, yelling at him to stop. Berry was hitting Mother harder and harder with his fist. Sissy and I took off running out of the house.

This time, when we got outside and ran for the cornfield next to our house, we noticed a police car with its lights on at a neighbor's house a little way down the highway. We knew that policemen could help. So I told Sissy to follow me, and I started running down the driveway. We got to the highway and ran right down the middle of it, with no shoes and in our nightgowns. Sissy ran faster than I did, so she took the lead. We were screaming for help and waving our hands above our heads. But the police car drove down the neighbor's driveway and then pulled onto the highway and drove off in the opposite direction. As it drove off, everything seemed to be in slow motion. Our neighbors were still outside and heard us yelling. They ran toward us. "Hurry! Get off the highway!" they said. We were relieved that we had gotten someone's attention.

We made it to their front yard. We were out of breath but tried to tell them what was going on. "Huh, huh, my, huh, dad is, huh, is beating my, huh, mother! Please, huh, help us, huh," I said, gasping for air. I did not know the man's or woman's name; however, it just so happened that the woman's father was the justice of the peace, and he lived a couple of houses over from them.

"Come on, sweeties. Come with me," the woman said. The man and woman walked us into their house. She walked us over to her couch and told us to sit down. She then walked over to her phone and called her father to ask him for help. We were relieved that we had gotten help, but we were also still terrified and shaking. We knew what was going on — we knew the horror that was taking place at our house. And we knew this time it was really bad. We feared for our mother's and our little sister's lives.

While Sissy and I sat on their couch, I looked around their living room with my tear-filled eyes. I began to wipe them. I looked at their happy family photos with their children. I thought, why is this happening to us? Why do we have to live like this?

The woman hung up the phone and sat down next to us. She told us that help was on the way. Sissy begged her to tell her father to hurry.

"He is, sweetheart," the woman said soothingly. "He will be here in a couple of minutes."

Back at our home, the beating continued, and Carrie was still trying to get Berry off of Mother. She tried to keep him from hitting and punching Mother. She tried to get him to stop. But she was so little that she was helpless. She knew that Berry was hitting mom too much and too hard this time. Mother also thought that this was going to be the night that Berry would end up killing her.

Mother kept telling Carrie to get her car keys out of her purse. She thought Berry was going to kill her, and she did not want Carrie to witness her death, so she kept urging her little girl to go look in her purse in the next room. Carrie didn't respond to mother; her full attention was on getting Berry to stop. Carrie refused to leave Mother's side.

Berry grabbed the yellow phone handset from the kitchen wall and struck mother in the head with it. A huge knot quickly rose in the middle of her forehead, and she fell down on the floor in the kitchen, unconscious. Mother was only unconscious for a few seconds. She opened her eyes slowly. Berry was relentless. He just kept hitting, slapping, and punching her. He got on his knees and straddled Mother's torso. He started to wrap the long yellow phone cord around her neck. Mother bent her knees and put her feet on the floor, trying to scoot on her back to get underneath the dining room table. She looked over at Carrie, who was grabbing Berry's arm, trying to stop him from wrapping the phone cord around Mom's neck. Mother said again to Carrie, "Baby, please go get my car keys out of my purse."

Carrie was crying, and she replied back to Mom this time, "I'm sorry, Mommy, I can't."

"Baby, please, Mommy needs her car keys," Mother pleaded. But Carrie started hitting and punching Berry with her little fists.

Back up the highway, where Sissy and I waited for the woman's father to arrive, time was standing still. It seemed to be taking a very long time for the man to get there. Finally, there was a knock at their front door.

The justice of the peace came inside and looked at us, sitting on the couch in our bare feet and nightgowns. "Let's go," he said to the man and woman.

We got into the justice of the peace's car with them and pulled out of their driveway. I pointed the way to our house. It was less than a quarter of a mile down the road, but it felt like ten miles. The justice of the peace turned into our driveway, and Sissy and I started to cry again. All kinds of thoughts ran through our little minds. Was Mommy okay? Was Carrie okay? Did Berry hurt them really bad? Also, the worst thought of all: are we too late?

We all got out of the car, but the woman held our hands and told us to stay outside with her for a minute and let the men go in first. Sissy and I stood there, holding the woman's hands as we watched her husband and father knock on our front door. There was no answer. The justice of the peace then started banging loudly on the door. "It's the justice of the peace," he announced and started banging again. Berry opened the front door.

"I'm the justice of the peace," the man repeated, "and I understand we have a problem here."

"No, we don't have a problem. It was just a little misunderstanding. Everything is okay now," Berry said.

"May we come in?"

"Sure," Berry replied, letting them inside.

Mother was in the bathroom with Carrie, wiping the blood off her face and mouth. Berry had told her to get up when he heard the banging on the front door.

"Where is your wife?" the justice of the peace asked.

"Katrina!" Berry called.

Mother walked into the living room, holding Carrie's hand, and whimpered hello.

The justice of the peace looked at mom and said, "Boy, that's a dinger." He knew that Berry had beat her, but back in the day, no one really said or did much of anything about domestic violence. The justice of the peace looked at mother and asked, "Are you okay?"

"Yes," Mother replied.

"Just a minute," the justice of the peace said. He walked over to the front door and opened it, motioning to his daughter to bring us in.

"Come on, sweeties," she said. Still holding our hands, she walked us into the house. Once inside, she looked at Berry and then over at Mother. She said to both of them, "Y'all need to stop this. Your two little girls here were running down the middle of the highway, and they could have been hit by a vehicle. It's way past their bedtime, and they should be asleep."

"Let's turn it down a notch or two and keep it down, okay?" the justice of the peace said to Mom and Berry.

"Sure thing," Berry said. Mom remained silent.

"Okay then," the justice of the peace added, as he and his daughter and son-in-law walked over to the front door and let themselves out, closing the door behind them.

Berry gave Mom a mean look and shook his head, as if everything had been my mother's fault. He walked by her, puffing his chest at her as he passed. He walked into the master bedroom and slammed the door shut.

Mother looked at us and told us it was time to get back to bed. She put Carrie in bed with me on the top bunk, sandwiched between me and the wall. Mother laid in the bottom bunk with Sissy. As the four of us lay there in those two small bunk beds, I heard Mother begin to cry. I fell asleep to the sound of my mom sobbing.

CHAPTER SIX

Grandparents Make Everything Better

Berry was working a full week every week, and he had been for a while now. He had also stopped drinking. Fall was upon us, and we had invited all of Mom's sisters, brothers, and their kids over to have a big cookout. They all arrived in the afternoon. Mother set up bases around the big triangle part of our front yard, on one side of our long driveway. All of my cousins, aunts, uncles, Mom, my sisters, and I divided up into two teams for a baseball game. We began to play ball. Each of us got a turn to bat. When our team went into the outfield, we all had our positions to play. It was a lot of fun and laughs. Berry lit the grill up in the backyard and put chicken on to cook. Mother made several pitchers of sweet tea. She also put snacks out for everyone.

Some of my aunts and uncles chose to drink beer, so they had brought their own. I was sure hoping that Berry was not going to start drinking. I kept asking him, "Dad, do you want a glass of tea?" Each time his response was "no, thanks."

As the afternoon started turning into early evening, Berry started drinking some of the beer. He was getting drunk — very drunk. I had found a big toad and walked over to him with it. I said, "Look, Dad!" He looked down at it, picked it up out of my hand and put it in his mouth.

"Uhh, Dad, you just put a toad in your mouth," I said numbly.

He puffed out his cheeks and took the toad out and handed it back to me. It was all wet and gross. I apologized to the toad and let it go on the ground.

Berry got so drunk while everyone was still there that he went into his bedroom and passed out. I guess it had taken a toll on him since he hadn't had anything to drink in months, and also, he would not dare try to hit my mother while her family was around.

It got dark and was getting late. Everyone left and went home. Mother took us inside the house and bathed us. She tucked Sissy and me into our beds. Carrie went into Mother's bedroom with her to sleep. Carrie slept with Mother and Berry. Mother and Berry had not been intimate since Carrie had been born. Berry slept on one side of the bed, mother in the middle, and Carrie on the other side of mom.

Right before Carrie was born, Berry had said he wanted a boy really bad. He had told Mother that if she had another girl, he was going to leave her. So when Carrie was born, Mother would not hold Carrie. Carrie stayed in the nursery, and she got very sick. Mother had gotten very worried and scared, and she told the nurse on duty to please bring Carrie to her. And from that moment on, Mother did not want to leave Carrie's side. And she didn't, unless she was at work.

As Sissy and I laid in our beds, we talked about the events that had happened earlier in the afternoon and laughed about some as we recalled them. We played a few rounds of the game "I spy." We were starting to get sleepy and said goodnight to each other. I laid there for a moment more, and all of a sudden, I saw a bunch of red dots — small red circles — all clustered together. They were floating across our bedroom. "Sissy, do you see all the red dots?" I asked. She did not answer; she had fallen asleep.

The cluster of red dots moved closer to our beds and then stopped right next to Sissy. I had my head over the side of my top bunk, looking down at the red dots. In height, the cluster was about five feet tall. It remained stationary beside Sissy's bed for a few seconds. "What in the world is that?" I whispered. The cluster suddenly moved upward, and I quickly pulled back and laid my head on my pillow. I closed my eyes but left them cracked just a bit so that I could still see out of them. The cluster of red dots moved up over the top of me. It stayed stationary over me for a few seconds. It then moved over to the right of me and straight into the wall next to my top bunk. The cluster of red dots disappeared into the wall. I couldn't stop thinking about it. Looking back, I can remember it as if it were yesterday, but I still do not know what it was. The only possibility I could think of was that it was the ghost.

The next morning, mother woke us up. She made us breakfast, and after we ate, she took us to visit Mama Carson, and then we were all going to head over to see our Grandma and Grandpa Smith. We arrived at Mama Carson's house. We got out of Mother's car and ran into Mama Carson's house. We walked over to Mama Carson and hugged her. She was talking to my Aunt Cassie, so we hugged her as well. Aunt Cassie had my cousin Mary with her. Mary had also come to see Mama Carson. And she wanted to see Grandma and Grandpa Smith too. Aunt Cassie had stopped by my uncle's house to visit him earlier in the day, and when she had started to leave, Mary wanted to go with her. Uncle Tom said it was okay if Aunt Cassie did not mind. She did not mind one bit.

After our visit with Mama Carson, Sissy and I asked Mom if it would be okay if we rode to Grandma and Grandpa Smith's with Aunt Cassie. She said it was okay, so we got into Aunt Cassie's orange car.

We drove down white rock roads that did not have any traffic on them, as we were way out in the country. Aunt Cassie was always loads of fun and loved kids. She never had any of her own, so she spoiled us. We could talk to her about anything and everything. "Do y'all want to take turns driving?" she asked us. Of course, we did!

Aunt Cassie pulled the car over and let our cousin Mary drive first. Mary sat behind the wheel and scooted forward to reach the gas pedal. Aunt Cassie told Mary, "This is the gear shift: this is park; this is drive; this is neutral; and this is reverse. This pedal is for the gas, and this one is the brakes."

"Okay, I got it," Mary responded, so Aunt Cassie gave Mary the go ahead to gently press on the gas pedal. I don't know if Mary slipped, but she hit the gas pedal so hard that we all flew back into our seats.

"Okay, that was good," Aunt Cassie encouraged. "Now it's Kristine's turn." Mary put the car in park, and Sissy got behind the wheel.

Sissy drove like she knew exactly what to do. She scooted up to reach the gas pedal, put the gear shift in drive, and gently pressed the gas pedal. She drove in a straight line down the road. We were just cruising down the road, and I was thinking that Sissy was such a good driver.

Aunt Cassie let her drive a little way down the road, and then it was my turn. I got behind the wheel and didn't have to scoot quite as far up as Mary and Sissy did. My legs were longer. I put the gear shift in drive, and we were cruising down the road once again. Wow! This was so much fun!

Aunt Cassie also let me drive a little way down the road, and then she had me stop so that she could drive us the rest of the way to our grandma and grandpa's house. We arrived at their house. We couldn't wait to tell Mother that we had gotten to drive Aunt Cassie's car. We ran into the house yelling, "Mom! Mom! We drove Aunt Cassie's car!"

"You did?" she smiled.

"Yes," Sissy and I both shouted. "Yes, and it was so much fun!"

Mother looked at Aunt Cassie and added, "I bet it was," while she was still smiling.

"It was not bad; they are really pretty good little drivers," Aunt Cassie said.

Grandpa Smith was sitting in his chair in the living room, and we walked over to him and gave him hugs and kisses. We turned around and ran into the kitchen where Mama Carson was talking to Grandma Smith. We hugged Grandma Smith and give her kisses too. Grandma Smith had an old, big metal ladle that she had hanging next to her kitchen sink. We grabbed a dining room chair and pushed it over to the sink. Mary, Sissy, and I took turns filling the ladle up with water and drinking it. When we were all done, we pushed the chair back over to the table. We went outside to play.

Grandma and Grandpa Smith's house was an old Victorian-style. It was probably built in the late 1800s or the early 1900s. Grandma and Grandpa had put up screens all the way around the side porch, and sometimes in the summer, Mother would let us spend the night with them, and we would sleep on little cots on the screened-in porch. It was amazing. Spending time with Grandma and Grandpa Smith made us so happy. It was always fun and so peaceful there.

Grandpa Smith played poker with some men downtown. Downtown was a hop, skip, and jump from their house. Grandpa walked there every Thursday to play cards. One summer afternoon, while we were there staying a few nights with them, I saw grandpa start walking toward town, and I followed him. About halfway there, he turned around and saw me on his tail. I was busted! "What are you doing?" he asked.

"I am going where you are going," I said.

"Child, you can't go where I am going. I won't be that long. Please go back home."

I did what he asked and turned around and went back to their house. I was so sad that I could not go with Grandpa that I walked into the house and told Grandma what had happened. Grandma picked me up and sat me on her lap. "Oh honey, you don't want to go where he is going," she told me. "It's just a bunch of old men, sitting around a table acting silly."

I got up and found my Sissy playing on the screened-in porch. She was playing with baby dolls. I started playing with her. I guess my grandpa felt guilty about leaving me to go play cards with his friends because the next day he made it up to me. He walked out on the front porch. He walked over to his rocking chair and sat down in it. Next to his rocking chair was a yellow meat watermelon. He called me while I was playing in the front yard with their old, small black dog named Mutt. "Come here, child," Grandpa called out to me. I walked up to him on the porch. "Do you want some of this watermelon?"

"Yes, please, Grandpa," I said.

He reached into his pants pocket and pulled out his pocket knife. I stood beside him and watched him cut the watermelon into two halves. He picked me up and sat me on his lap. He held onto me with one hand and arm while he leaned over and picked up one of the watermelon halves with his pocket knife still stuck in it. He used his knife to cut small squares out of the watermelon half. He cut me a bite of it and then he cut him one. We sat there in his rocking chair, and we ate that whole half of the yellow meat watermelon. This was the life! We all said goodbye to Grandma and Grandpa Smith. We headed home.

Mama Carson was the daughter of Grandma and Grandpa Smith. She was my mother's mother. I loved my Mama Carson. Whenever there was trouble, Mama Carson came. We also went to stay nights with Mama Carson, and there was never a dull moment. She kept us on our toes. She had chickens and roosters outside in her yard. We always had fresh eggs and chickens to eat. Yes, fresh chickens to eat!

While my sisters, cousins, and I played in her big yard, Mama Carson would walk out to her chicken coop after lunch and pick out a chicken. Sometimes she grabbed the chicken by the neck, swinging it in a circular motion until the chicken's head came off. The headless chicken body would then flip and flop around on the ground until it stopped and did not move anymore. Mama Carson would then pick up the headless chicken and take it inside her house. She would run smoking hot water in her kitchen sink and put the headless chicken in there to soak. Later, she would drain the hot water and pluck all the feathers off the chicken.

It was kinda a gruesome scene for small children to watch and witness, but I guess Mama Carson was just doing what she knew, what she was taught, and what she had witnessed as a child.

Sometimes she would lay the chicken down on the ground and step on the chicken's head and neck. She would then twist the chicken's body fast and pull the chicken's head off that way. No matter the technique she used, the outcome was always the same for the chicken: it was dead, and it was dinner in Mama Carson's frying pan that night.

The fresh eggs she got from her chickens were very good. Sometimes while we stayed with Mama Carson, she would have us go into the chicken coop and gather the eggs. I remember the first time she told me to go get the eggs. I walked to the chicken coop and opened the door latch. I closed it behind me. I walked over to the wooden door and went inside the wooden shed where the chickens had their own sectioned-off nests with hay in them. I noticed that a couple of chickens were still sitting on their nests. I gathered all the eggs from the empty nests. And then I looked at the chicken next to me, still sitting on her nest. I said to it, "I have come to gather the eggs." The chicken looked at me, and she cackled an evil, mean cackle, as if she were warning me to just try to take her eggs. I was scared of her, but I wanted to show my Mama Carson that I was a big girl, so I slowly moved my hand toward the chicken. As my hand got up close to the chicken, she started pecking at my hand. Heck no, I thought to myself, and I pulled my hand away and went outside. I found a long stick. I walked back into the chicken coop toward that chicken. I swung the stick and hit the chicken, not hard, but I let her know who was boss. It scared her, and she moved quickly off the nest. And every time after that, when I gathered the eggs, I took a stick with me into the chicken coop, and if there were any chickens still sitting on their eggs in their nests, they moved off quickly. If my Mama Carson had known about that, what I was doing with that stick, she probably would have taken that stick and spanked my bobo with it.

Mama Carson gave me a chicken of my own. It was a pretty one, not your average white one. This one was gray-ish brown and small. She stayed in the barn out back at night, and she would come out of the barn in the morning and roam around the yard until it was night again. One morning I went out to see her and feed her. She had some-thing very small next to her. It was following her around. As I approached her, I thought, what in the world is that? I reached her. It was a baby chicken, a gray one. It was so tiny. I bent down and said, "Hello, little baby." I was so excited that I ran into the house. I called Mama Carson and told her that I had a baby chicken.

"You do?" she asked.

"Yes!" I said. "And it is so cute!"

Mama Carson brought me some baby chicken food. She walked to the barn with me and saw the baby chick. She said, "Well I'll be. It sure is a baby chicken." She sprinkled some of the baby chicken food on the ground. It would not eat. The hen started to eat a little of it. But the baby would not. "Let's leave them alone," Mama Carson said. "I'm sure the baby will eat when we leave." We walked away.

Mama Carson left the bag of baby chicken food with me, and I went out to see it the next morning. It was in the barn with its mama. I walked into the barn and sprinkled some food for it and fed the mama. The hen ate all of her food, but the baby would not eat. I stood there and watched the baby chick standing next to its mother. I said, "Baby, you have to eat." I sat down on the dirt in the barn. I was watching the baby chick when suddenly I heard footsteps approach me in the dirt. I looked all around, thinking it might be one of my sisters or my mother, even though I knew the footstep sound was coming from inside the barn and I saw no one. I then heard breathing. Nobody was there; however, I clearly heard footsteps walking in the barn, shuffling in the dirt, and I heard someone breathing.

I jumped up as fast as I could and ran as fast as I could out of the barn. I got Sissy to go back to the barn with me the next day to feed the mama and baby chicken. When we made it to the barn, I saw the mama but not the baby chicken. I said, "Where is my baby chick at?" Sissy and I walked into the barn together. I looked around. I spotted the baby chick. It lay dead, in the very same spot where I had left it when I ran out of the barn the day before when I had heard the footsteps and breathing. I looked at Sissy and I said, "Let's go. Let's get out of here." My chicken also disappeared a couple of days later. I never found her.

CHAPTER SEVEN

Coming of Age ... Country Style

Growing up, my sisters and I did not have a lot of toys to play with. So, we were innovative. We came up with games to play, and we made stuff to play with. There was a line of thin-trunk willow trees in the backyard. My sisters and I would bend one over and voila! We had a bucking horse or bull! We would take turns sitting on the middle of the tree trunk while one of us held onto the tree top with both hands and moved the tree up and down, making a bucking motion. It was loads of fun.

Carrie had a little red wagon, and she had her dog, Charlie Brown. We took an old table out of the storage shed in the backyard. It was the perfect size — the table legs slid right into the wagon. Our goal was to make a covered wagon like the ones that horses pulled in the pioneer days. I went into the house and got a little white sheet out of the storage closet. Sissy helped me put it over the table. It was the perfect size to cover the table. Sissy decided that we also needed a horse to pull us in the wagon. We looked around, wondering what could become our horse. "Charlie Brown can be our horse," Carrie suggested.

"That's perfect," I agreed. I went into the garage and found a couple of small ropes. I told Sissy and Carrie to hold onto Charlie Brown in front of the wagon. I took the rope and tied it to Charlie Brown's collar. I then took the other end of the rope and tied it to the handle on the wagon. I tied the second, longer rope around Charlie Brown's torso. As I finished tying the ropes, Sissy was already sitting on the top of the table, and Carrie was underneath the table and white sheet. I handed Sissy the rope that was attached to Charlie Brown's torso. She took the rope from me and she waved the rope, saying, "Giddy up!" I was and I'm pretty sure my sisters were thinking and expecting Charlie Brown to go and pull them in the wagon, but he didn't. He just stood there looking around, with his tongue hanging out, panting.

"Sissy, let me try," I said. "I think I can get him to go."

Sissy climbed down off the top of the sheet-covered tabletop. I climbed up on it. I grabbed the rope. I shook it and said, "Giddy up, Charlie Brown!" We were still not moving. We decided to just pull each other around in the covered wagon. We untied Charlie Brown. He ran off and laid under a pecan tree.

Berry brought home a baby brown pig. My sisters and I thought it would be a neat pet, and we named her Pebbles.

Berry built some fencing around the back of the barn. He then cut an opening in the back of the barn so that Pebbles could go into the barn to take shelter in storms. We loved Pebbles. We played so much with her when she was little. She began to grow, and when she got big enough, we started climbing onto her back and riding her around. As she kept growing and got really big, we stopped riding her. She got mean — very mean.

Sissy and I had each gotten a pair of cowboy boots for Christmas. Mine were black with red trimmings around the boots. Sissy's were all brown. Carrie had one of her school friends over one afternoon. It had been raining. The yard was muddy, but Pebbles' pigpen behind the barn was *really* muddy. Carrie and her friend Ellen put on the new boots that Sissy and I had gotten for Christmas. They went outside to play in the backyard. Carrie wanted to show Ellen how big Pebbles had gotten. They walked over to the back of the barn where the pigpen was. They peeped through the wooden fence. Pebbles was nowhere around. Carrie called for Pebbles. Pebbles did not come. Carrie said to Ellen, "Come on, let's climb over the fence and look for her." They climbed over the fence and landed feet first in the sticky, sinking mud in our brand new boots. Carrie called out for Pebbles again, and this time they heard Pebbles grunt and squeal loudly as she came charging around the corner of the barn.

Carrie and Ellen tried to move their feet in our boots, but they were sunken in the mud and were stuck. Carrie and Ellen jumped out of our boots, turned around, and ran toward the fence. They climbed to the top of the fence in the nick of time, just before Pebbles reached them. To this very day, our boots are stuck, buried in the dirt, exactly where Carrie and Ellen had left them.

One evening, mother cooked something different. She cooked ham steaks. We sat down at the dinner table. I said, "Yummy! My favorite, ham!" We started to eat our ham dinner. "Mom, this is so good," I added.

"You like the taste of Pebbles?" Berry asked. I had a mouthful of the ham, and I spit it out on my plate. My sisters and I started crying.

"This ham is Pebbles?" I said between sobs. Sissy and Carrie spit theirs out onto their plates too.

"Yes," Berry said, getting up from the table. He walked over to the icebox and opened it. Inside the freezer was a bunch of different sized white paper packages.

"How could you do that?" Sissy said. "How could you kill our pet pig and feed it to us?"

We could tell that Mother immediately felt really bad. We ended up not eating any more of Pebbles. Mother and Berry gave what was left of her to a family member. Berry and Mother had purchased Pebbles for that one purpose only: to put food on our dinner table because we were poor, but my sisters and I were not going to eat our pets.

We used to help Berry gather pecans from the pecan trees around the house. Berry would put sheets all around and underneath the big pecan trees. He would climb each tree and then jump up and down on the branches. The pecans would fall onto the sheets and also all around on the ground. My sisters and I would walk around and pick up the pecans that did not fall on the sheets. We picked them up and threw them on the sheets. After we were all done gathering the pecans from all the pecan trees in the yard, Berry would take us to a shop in town that bought the pecans from us. As soon as the man paid him for the pecans, Berry would then pay us each a whole dollar for helping him.

One day on the way home from selling the pecans, I wanted to buy some ice cream sandwiches with my money. Berry stopped at the store, and I bought a box with my dollar. We got back home, but the icebox freezer was too full of the vegetables that Mama Carson had picked from her garden and had given to mother. So, we took the ice cream sandwiches to the garage and put them in the big chest freezer that Berry had bought somewhere cheap. Sissy and I stood out in the garage eating our ice cream sandwiches. I looked to the side of me, at a garage shelf. The sheets that Berry used to gather the pecans were stored there. I said, "Sissy, I have a great idea."

"What?" she asked, taking the last bite of her ice cream.

"Let's put you up on top of my shoulders and then put these sheets around you."

"Why?" Sissy wondered, putting the plastic straw she had been holding in her hand into her mouth. Sissy loved to chew on straws. Berry had also stopped on the way home to get each of us a soda. Sissy had thrown her cup away but had kept the straw to chew on.

"We can scare Carrie. She'll think we are a monster!"

"That is a great idea!" Sissy replied.

I took the sheets off the shelf. She was behind me chewing on her straw. I started to turn around to hand her a sheet, and somehow my elbow hit Sissy's straw and pushed it into the back of her throat. She immediately started choking. I turned fully around to face her, not knowing what I had done. I looked at her and said, "What's wrong Sissy?" Her mouth was wide open, and I could see the long straw sticking out from the back of her throat. I started screaming that I had killed my Sissy! I ran into the house, screaming to mother, "I killed my Sissy!"

Mother panicked, putting her hand on her chest, and said, "What happened? Where is Kristine?"

I was crying so hard. "I killed her in the garage." Mother and I ran out to the garage. We both looked over at Sissy, who had sat down on a wooden chair in the garage next to where we had been standing. Her mouth was still hanging open, and the straw was still sticking out of her throat. She was still making the choking sound. Mother ran over to her and scooped her up quickly but gently. She took Sissy and put her in the car. Mother turned around and told me to get her purse. I ran inside the house as fast as I could and then ran back outside to hand my mother her purse. Mother quickly pulled her car keys from her purse and said to me, "Julie, go tell your dad that I am taking Kristine to the hospital."

"I am so sorry, Mom. I didn't mean to kill her," I cried.

"You did not kill her," she said. "But I have to take her to the doctor now to get the straw out of her throat." I watched as my mother put the car in reverse, turned it around, and then drove down the driveway. When she reached the highway, she sped off quickly.

I went inside the house to tell Berry what had happened. He looked at me and said, "Kristine will be fine."

It seemed to take forever, but several hours later, Mother returned home with my Sissy. She was okay and thank goodness the straw only went into her throat a little bit. It went in far enough to poke a hole in the back of her throat the size of the straw, but it didn't go deep enough into her throat to hurt her badly. I walked up to Sissy and looked at her. I told her how sorry I was, and I hugged her. I looked at mom and I said, "I did not kill my Sissy."

"No, you did not," Mother replied back. "But you have to be very careful playing with your sisters."

"I will be very, very careful from now on." I was so scared that I was shaking. I had thought that I had actually killed my Sissy. And I was so relieved to know that I hadn't. I could not have lived without my Sissy. She was my sister and my best friend.

CHAPTER EIGHT

No More Little White Tin House

As we grew and got older, Berry had stopped drinking, hitting, and beating my mother. We also had not seen or heard anything from the ghost in the little white tin house for a long time.

And when I reached the eighth grade in school, Berry and mother had enough money to buy a brand new double-wide mobile home. We all went as a family to pick one out. We looked at several different places. We finally found one. It was perfect for us. That meant that the little white tin house had to be moved off of our land. Someone that I do not know bought the little white tin house. They paid movers to move it off of our property and then up the highway to their property. Our property looked so different without the little white tin house there.

A day after the little tin house was moved to another property, our brand new double-wide mobile home arrived, in two halves. "How is this going to work?" I asked. Mother explained to me that some men would set it up in the very same spot where our other house was and then seal the two parts together.

In just a couple of days, our home was ready for us to move into. Yay! We were ready. We had been staying the last several nights with Mama Carson. The new home was completely furnished. It had everything, and it was nice. It had three bedrooms and an extra bathroom, which we were very happy about. No more waiting on someone in the bathroom — when you gotta go, you gotta go!

Our new home had two full bathrooms, a big living room, a good-sized kitchen, a dining room, and a utility room. It had carpet throughout, except in the kitchen, the bathrooms, and the utility room. We were so excited to be living in our new home! Sissy shared a room with Carrie right next to my room. Their room was a little bigger than mine because they had to share. I was the oldest, so mother let me have a room of my own. The master bedroom was down a long hall and through the living room, on the opposite side of the double-wide from our rooms. Everything seemed so perfect. We were a happier family. We had a new house with no ghost in it. I had absolutely no idea what was coming next. What seemed so great would all of a sudden turn scary, really quick. I guess the ghost got really mad that we had sold and then moved its house away. And I guess it wanted to stay behind, with us, to let us know just how livid it was. Everything was so wonderful until the night when the terror began in our new home.

It was the weekend. Mother did not work on the weekends. We had been asking her to have a slumber party with us — just us girls and Mother. We wanted to stay up as late as we could and eat snacks and watch movies. On that Friday, mother was too tired to have the slumber party with us, but she said we could have the slumber party on Saturday night. Mother made popcorn, we had sodas to drink, and I'm sure there was chocolate involved, as we were all chocoholics.

My sisters and I made our own pallets on the floor in the living room. Mother laid on the couch. We put all of our snacks and drinks on the coffee table. Mother turned on the TV and found a really funny movie for us to watch. We laughed so hard we cried tears. We watched two more movies. I was getting so sleepy. I don't remember falling asleep, but I do remember being awakened by the sound of someone beating on the front door. The wind was blowing hard outside. I could hear the wind, but the banging on the front door was much louder. It scared me. The lamp in the living room was on. I looked over and saw my two sisters lying on their pallets, and my mother was fast asleep on the couch. My pallet was close to Mother. I sat up and touched Mother and gently shook her. "Mom, someone is beating on the door," I whispered.

She looked at me and sat up. She listened. There was nothing. "It's the wind, Julie." Mother laid back down and so did I. I thought that Mother must have been right and that it was just the wind.

But as soon as Mother had fallen back to sleep and I had closed my eyes ... BOOM! BOOM! BOOM! Frightened, I sat up and touched Mother once again, gently shaking her.

"It's back, the banging on the door," I whispered again, not wanting to wake my sisters.

Mother sat up again and listened. Nothing. She looked at me and collapsed back onto the couch. "Julie, it's nothing. It's just the wind. Please go to sleep."

I laid back down on my pallet. As soon as Mother fell asleep again ... BOOM! BOOM! BOOM! This time, I looked at the front door as soon as the pounding started, and I could see the front door move as it got banged on. It was so loud. It seemed and sounded like someone or something was trying to kick the front door in. I laid there and covered up my head and peeked out of the covers. I just knew that at any minute the front door would be kicked in. My mother never woke up to the loud banging noise on the front door. My sisters never woke up, and Berry, in the master bedroom asleep, never woke up. I laid there, listening to that banging and beating on the front door, scared and terrified for hours, until I finally drifted off.

The following week, I came home from school, walked into the house, and went straight into the kitchen. I opened the icebox and grabbed the carton of milk. I opened it and started chugging it. The icebox door was open with my one hand on it. This was my routine every day after school. I loved milk, and I was always thirsty when I got home from school. The milk had been good and fresh the day before when I had gotten home from school. But when I opened it and started drinking it on that particular day, something was different. It was thick going down my throat and tasted awful. I sat the milk carton back down inside the icebox and started to turn around when the loaf of bread sitting on the kitchen cabinet, next to the icebox, raised straight up off the cabinet about a foot and then dropped back down. Bile started coming up my throat. I made a mad dash for the back door, and as soon as I opened it, I threw up everywhere. I walked back into the kitchen and looked at the loaf of bread sitting there on the cabinet. No way did that just happen, I thought to myself and shrugged it off. Boy was I wrong.

I was not the only one experiencing scary stuff. My Sissy experienced some scary stuff too. One day during the week she wanted to play hooky. She played sick that morning, and Mother let her stay home. Carrie and I got on the bus and went to school. Sissy was all by herself in the house. She thought it would be great to eat whatever she wanted and have the TV all to herself.

Once the house was empty, she went into the kitchen and got some cereal. She walked into the living room and turned on the TV. She sat on the couch eating her cereal while she watched TV. She finished her cereal and sat her bowl down on the coffee table. After only an hour of being by herself, she heard loud scratching, and it was coming from her bedroom closet. She was getting a little scared, but tried to brush it off as something natural, explainable, like maybe squirrels in the attic. She had gotten up to investigate the noise but decided to sit back down and watch TV again. The scratching in her closet got louder and louder, and then she heard a huge crashing sound so loud that it rattled the house and windows.

She was still in her pajamas, but she got up off the couch, ran out the front door, and climbed onto a wooden picnic table that Berry had made, which was sitting between two tall pecan trees in the front yard.

At three thirty that afternoon, when Carrie and I arrived home on the bus, I saw Sissy. She was outside in her pajamas, sitting on the picnic table. Carrie and I walked up the driveway. Sissy got up off the picnic table and walked over to us. "Sissy, what are you doing sitting out here on the picnic table in your pajamas?" I asked.

She told us what had happened, adding, "I was not about to stay in that house. I stayed out here in my pajamas all day."

Sissy was so thirsty and hungry, and while we were scared to go into the house, we were much braver together. We entered the house cautiously and went into the kitchen. Sissy got a glass out of the cabinet and filled it with cold water from the kitchen faucet and drank it fast. We then went slowly down the hall together. We peeked into her room. Sissy was standing behind me. I reached around the wall and turned on her bedroom light. We walked into the bedroom, inching slowly, shuffling our feet on the floor. Sissy was still behind me as I made my way toward her sliding closet doors. I slid one door open. There was nothing. Nothing was messed up in her closet. Sissy looked at me and said, "I am not lying to you. There was loud scratching and then there was this loud crash."

I looked at Sissy and said, "I believe you."

CHAPTER NINE

Seeing is Believing

As the days passed and scary, unexplainable things continued to happen, we tried to tell mother that something was going on. She did not believe us, and she had an explanation for each incident that had taken place.

We told her about the time that both Sissy's and my beds shook — in different rooms at different times. It had felt as if someone had walked up to my bed, put their hands on the mattress, and then shook it back and forth. Mother's explanation was that it was just the house settling.

I told Mother to come into my bedroom so I could show her what I was talking about. I walked over to my bed and shook it with my hand. "The house settles like this?" I asked her, as I kept shaking my mattress.

Mother looked at me, "Yes."

"No way," I replied. "The house moves like this?"

She insisted that it did. I said okay, but I doubted her response. Neither Sissy nor I was convinced.

Just one week after our beds had been shaken, we heard someone or something with two feet walking down the hallway on the carpet toward our bedrooms. Mother always slept with a fan on in her room. She had already gone to bed and was asleep. It was silent in the house, so the footsteps were very distinctive. The footsteps stopped at the end of the hallway, next to our bedrooms. It was pitch black in the house. "Sissy, is that you?" I asked her.

"No. Is that you?" she responded.

"No," I answered. Chills ran all up and down my spine, and I heard Sissy gasp in fear. "On the count of three, we get up and turn on our lights at the same time," I said. Sissy agreed and I counted. When I reached three, we both jumped up and ran toward our light switches, smacking our hands on the wall when they made contact. We both looked out our bedroom doors. "Do you want to leave your bedroom light on with my bedroom light on, and you can sleep in my bedroom with me?" I asked her. We did just that. We left both lights on, and Sissy slept with me in my bedroom that night.

On nights when Sissy stayed with her friends for sleepovers, I started sleeping in the living room. I would turn on the TV and fall asleep with it on. For some reason, I thought I would be safe there. Nope! I was wrong. One night while

Sissy was spending the night at a friend's house, I took my blanket and pillow into the living room. I put my pillow and blanket on the couch and watched TV until I fell asleep. In the middle of the night, I was awakened by something tugging at my pillow. Carrie had gotten a new puppy, Shag, and she kept him in the house. Every time Mother and Carrie gave him a bath, he would run up and down the couch, rubbing himself on it. When I felt the tugging on my pillow, I thought it was Shag. "Stop it, Shag," I said sleepily, as I waved my hand down low to shoo him away.

I fell back to sleep, but just a few minutes later it happened again. This time, my pillow had been tugged and pulled almost all the way off the couch. I looked around the living room, but I didn't see Shag anywhere. I told myself that I must have been tossing and turning too much, and that's why my pillow was on the edge of the couch. I shoved my pillow back underneath my head and fell asleep.

Then, with one solid yank, my pillow was jerked out from under my head and thrown halfway across the living room. I got up and turned on the living room light, the hall light, and the kitchen light. I turned on all the lights that I could and sat on the couch. I didn't lie back down. I left my pillow in the middle of the living room floor, and I fell back to sleep sitting up on the couch.

The next morning, Mother came into the living room to wake me. "Why are all the lights on in the house, and what is your pillow doing in the middle of the floor? And why are you sleeping sitting up?"

"Mom, you're not going to believe me, but my pillow was tugged on, and then it got yanked out from under my head. And that is where it landed on the floor."

"Julie, you had a bad dream."

"If it was a bad dream, then how did my pillow get tossed across the room?"

"You threw it in your sleep," she said, and then she told me to help her turn off all the lights. I knew it was pointless to keep talking to her about what had actually happened, because no matter what I said to her, she wouldn't believe it. She was not experiencing what Sissy and I were experiencing, so how could she believe it was all real and true? These supernatural events only seemed to happen to me and Sissy. Whenever we had our cousins and friends over to stay the night, nothing would happen. Nothing ever happened to anyone else but Sissy and me. But that would soon change.

A month had passed since the "ghost" had thrown my pillow across the room, and things had been calm. I began to kinda, sorta, maybe believe what mother had said, that it was only a bad dream and that I had tossed my pillow myself. And maybe the house did do strange things when it was settling. Anything was possible, I supposed, so the very next time Sissy went to a friend's house to spend the night, I decided to sleep again in the living room with the TV on.

I was awakened again in the middle of the night, only this time, my face was being slapped hard. All I could think was why was Mom slapping me in the face? But when I opened my eyes, my mother was not standing there. No one was standing there. Yet my face hurt so badly. I had felt the slap. The pain was real. I did not dream it, and I most definitely did not slap myself in my own face.

I got up off the couch and took my blanket and pillow to my bedroom, turned on my bedroom light, and sat on my bed awake all night. When the sun came up, I fell asleep. I slept until noon, and when I woke up and got up out of bed, I walked into the living room where Mother was sitting. Mother looked at me and said, "Someone is a sleepy head." I didn't bother telling her anything about what I had experienced. I saw it pointless as she would not believe me at all. She would just tell me that it was another bad dream or something like that.

"I saved you a plate of breakfast, but if you prefer, I can make you a sandwich for lunch," she said.

"Breakfast sounds good. Thank you, Mom." I walked into the kitchen and picked up my plate of food. I walked back into the living room and sat down on the couch and ate the eggs, bacon, and toast that Mother had made for breakfast. When I finished eating, I took my empty plate into the kitchen and I hand washed it. We did not have a dishwasher. We were the dishwashers.

I went into my bedroom and got out the big silver jam box that I had gotten for my birthday present the month before. It had a mini TV in it. I carried it into Mother's master bathroom and sat it on a shelf near the deep garden tub. I went back to my bedroom to get my makeup bag.

I returned to the bathroom and turned on my jam box. I sat my makeup bag on Mother's vanity and ran some bath water. I took a nice relaxing bath while listening to music. When I had finished, I pulled up the stopper in the tub so the water could drain out, then I wrapped a towel around myself and stepped out of the tub. The music was still playing on my jam box as I dried myself off and put on my clean clothes. I sat down in Mother's vanity chair, and my heart thudded hard in my chest. On Mother's vanity top was all of my makeup, lined up perfectly in a straight line. My makeup had been taken out of my makeup bag, and each of my individual products had been lined up in a row. Someone or something had been in that bathroom with me. I was terrified. I left my makeup and jam box where they sat and went to the living room and sat with my mother. I felt safe with her.

Later that night, the ghost would finally show Mother that what Sissy and I had been trying to tell her all along was actually true.

Two months prior to the ghost finally showing itself to Mother, she had finally kicked Berry out. Berry had remained sober for several years, but all of a sudden, he had started drinking again. And Mother had been at her wit's end with him. She was finally done; she had had enough, and she wanted a divorce. She threw him out, and he had been staying next door with his father ever since.

Mom read a lot of books — that was her escape and relax time. She often stayed up late at night reading books in bed. Mother was in her bed reading when she heard scratching in her master bathroom. She looked up from her book and listened. The scratching stopped. She began reading again. The scratching started up again. She put her book in her lap, holding her place in the book with her fingers, and looked at the entrance of the bathroom. The scratching stopped again. I need to get some mouse traps and set them out, or maybe we have rats in the house, she thought to herself, and began reading again. All of a sudden, my heavy jam box flew across the bathroom and hit the wall on the other side of the bathroom, striking with such force that it made a loud boom and shattered into pieces.

Mother had washed clothes earlier in the day. She had folded and laid six pairs of her blue jeans right in front of my jam box on the shelf next to the garden tub. Mother was scared. She had no idea what had just happened in her bathroom, but she knew that it definitely was not rats. She got up out of bed and walked to the bathroom. She turned on the bathroom light. My jam box was completely destroyed, and her blue jeans were scattered across the bathroom floor. She left everything the way she found it and left the bathroom light on.

The very next morning, I walked into Mother's bathroom to get my jam box and makeup. Mother was in the kitchen making breakfast. I turned on the bathroom light, and I couldn't believe my eyes. My jam box was destroyed, and my mother's blue jeans were scattered everywhere. I was devastated.

I walked into the kitchen. "Mom, why did you break my jam box?"

"I didn't," she said somberly. And then she began to explain what had happened. She took me into her bedroom and reenacted everything, describing step-by-step what she had heard and how things had happened. "I am sorry about your jam box, and I am also sorry that I did not believe y'all before. There is definitely something going on."

That was my chance to tell her what had happened to me on the couch and I did. Mother looked very concerned. She hugged me. She said, "Everything is going to be okay." Later that night, Mother prayed. She prayed for God to please protect us and keep us safe. She prayed to God to please remove the ghost from our home.

CHAPTER TEN

Moving On

Across the yard, Berry sat and drank at his father's house, where he was living. It was the Fourth of July, and it was very hot outside. He had been over to our house a couple of times to try to sweet-talk Mom again, but this time was different. It had been months since she had kicked him out of our house, and Mother was sticking to her guns. He had no one to blame but himself.

He cursed Mother, lifting the can of beer to his lips as he sat in a chair in his father's garage. He blamed her for everything. Mother did not force Berry to drink beer, nor did she force him to hit her and beat her up. It was Berry's own fault for making bad decisions over and over. And I was so proud of my mother for standing firm. While Berry sat across the yard, inside his father's garage, drinking himself to death, my sisters and I walked down the highway to purchase some fireworks for the Fourth of July holiday.

There were so many colorful firecrackers to choose from, but we only had a certain amount of money. I let my sisters pick out some, and then I picked out a couple. We walked back down the highway to our house and asked Mother if she would shoot them off with us when it got dark. "Yes," she smiled.

As the hot afternoon sun started setting in the western sky, the daylight waned, and it was time to light the firecrackers. My sisters, Mother, and I walked out into the front yard. We emptied the sack of firecrackers onto the sidewalk. When the concrete had originally been poured, Kristine, Carrie, and I put our first initials at the end of the sidewalk with a stick. It read J K C.

Mother had a lighter to light the firecrackers. Carrie and I picked up some sparklers. They were pretty and fun. Sissy picked up some bottle rockets. They went straight up and made a loud boom when they exploded. We had to put them in soda bottles before we lit them. We were having so much fun together. We were laughing as we talked and shot off the firecrackers.

We were all gathered by Mother's parked car in the driveway when a bottle rocket whizzed close enough past me that it went right through my long blonde hair. "What was that?" I asked.

We all looked around, but we didn't see or hear anything. We continued to light firecrackers until we were interrupted by another bottle rocket. This time it hit Mother's car and exploded right next to Carrie. We looked in the direction the bottle rocket had come from — around the back corner of our house. Berry was peeking around the corner, laughing, and clearly very drunk. "Pick up the fire-crackers quickly. We're going inside," Mother said.

We walked quickly into our house, and Mother locked the doors. That made Berry mad, but he did not try to do anything else. He walked back over to his father's house. That night in bed, I thought to myself that the bottle rocket that had gone through my hair could have gotten tangled, and it could have exploded. If that had happened, it would have hurt me. And then I thought, if one of those bottle rockets that Berry shot off at us had hit one of my sisters and exploded, it would have hurt them too.

Berry continued to live with his father right next door. Days, weeks, and then a few years went by without an incident with Berry or the ghost. I graduated from high school in May and started looking for work. My cousin Mary was working at a restaurant. She knew that I needed a job, and it just so happened that the restaurant where she worked was hiring. Mary called me to tell me about the position at the restaurant. She also told me about this young man who looked like Vince Neil, who just so happened to be working there too. Mary knew that I had a crush on Vince Neil, who was the lead singer of the popular eighties band Mötley Crüe. Mary told me to apply as soon as possible and that she would tell the manager that her cousin was coming to apply for the position. I thanked Mary, and the very next morning, I went down to the restaurant and filled out an application. The manager hired me on the spot. I started work a few days later.

On my first day of work, I met the guy who looked like Vince Neil. He turned out to be a big disappointment, but at least I was happy to be earning a paycheck, so I happily kept the job.

For some reason, one particularly long work day seemed to drag. I guessed it was because I was tired and just wanted to get off my feet. Finally, the workday ended, and I was on my way home. Even the drive there seemed like it was taking forever, but I finally arrived.

I noticed right away that something was not quite right. I panicked as I looked at the cars parked in front of Mother's house. There is my uncle's truck and my aunt's car. But where is my mother's car? Oh dear God, what had happened? Fear filled my body from my head to my toes. I was so scared that my body started to shake. It was the same sense of fear and panic that I had known all-too well as a very young girl.

I pulled up the driveway, parked my car, and ran into Mother's house as fast as I could, yelling, "Mom!" At first, I didn't see anyone.

"Julie, in here," my aunt Cassie called to me. She was standing in the kitchen next to her boyfriend, Scott, and my uncle Tom. Uncle Tom had the back door cracked, and he was peeking out the door to the backyard. He was yelling to Berry to drop the gun.

Berry was sitting up in a tree holding his rifle, which had a scope on it and a strap attached to it. "Oh God, no!" I cried. All I could think was that Berry had Mom and my sisters out there with him. What had Berry done to them? Were they hurt? Were they out there with him? I didn't know what was going on, and all these thoughts were running through my mind. I did not know that Berry was all alone, sitting up in a tree, with his rifle.

I rushed to the back door where the others were standing. "Drop the gun, Berry!" Uncle Tom continued to yell.

Berry started to taunt Uncle Tom, holding the rifle strap and acting as if he was going to drop the rifle, saying, "Oops, oops," each time he lowered the rifle. Berry then actually dropped the rifle and tried to reach for it. He lost his balance and fell out of the tall pecan tree and landed on the ground.

Uncle Tom ran outside immediately and grabbed the rifle and handed it to Scott. I still don't know what came over me that day. I walked over to Berry, who was sitting up with his back against the tree trunk, and I started punching him in his face over and over as hard as I could. "You piece of crap! I put up with this the whole time I was growing up! I am not going to put up with this anymore!"

My uncle Tom walked over to me and said, "That's enough," as he tried to pull me away from Berry.

I continued to punch Berry in the face as I replied, "No! No, it is not enough!"

Uncle Tom pulled me away from Berry and turned me around. He looked at me and said, "Calm down; that is enough."

The police arrived a few minutes later and took Berry away in handcuffs. There were so many police cars in Mother's yard. I believed that every police car in the county was there that day. I walked back into the house with my aunt

Cassie. She looked at me and asked me if I was okay. I told her I was … somehow … I was okay.

Mother and Carrie returned home about thirty minutes later. I was so relieved to see them. "Where is Sissy?" I asked. Mother told me that Sissy was at a football game. "What happened?" I added. She began to tell me everything.

Berry had come over earlier that afternoon. He had walked into the house and then into the master bathroom, where Sissy was getting ready to go to the football game. Sissy was a cheerleader. She had been in the master bathroom curling her hair when he walked in. Berry had looked at Sissy as she was curling her hair and he had started knocking things off of the bathroom shelves. He was dressed in cutoff blue jean shorts. He was wearing tennis shoes and a white t-shirt, with a bandana tied around his head. He had blood and scratches on his legs and arms. Sissy had looked at him and, quickly unrolling the curling iron from her hair, she had said, "Daddy, why are you acting like this? I love you, Daddy."

Berry had looked at her and said, "They are after me. I ran and hid from the SWAT team. They almost got me, but I hid good." Berry then walked out of the master bathroom and went into the kitchen where Mother and Carrie were talking and making cookies together. He started yelling, "This kitchen is a freaking mess!" He walked over to a cabinet and got a large bowl out of it. He filled the bowl with water in the kitchen sink. He then started drinking the water out of the bowl. The water in the bowl started spilling all over him and the floor.

Carrie looked at him and said, "You're a freaking idiot." Berry walked over to Carrie and punched her in her mouth, breaking her front tooth. The force of the punch also knocked her backward onto the floor. Mother was in shock and also very angry. Her maternal instincts went into overdrive, and she started attacking Berry. She hit him and punched him.

Carrie sat up and put her hand on her mouth. She could feel her broken tooth, and she saw blood on her hand. She got up and walked over to Berry, who had Mother on the floor, beating her and hitting her. That little girl inside Carrie — that brave little girl who never ran away, who always stayed by Mother's side and tried to help Mother — that little girl came out of Carrie, and she was madder and stronger than ever before.

Carrie started punching Berry, and with each punch she screamed, "I am not scared of you! You can't hurt me!"

Sissy heard the fighting and screaming in the kitchen. She put her shoes on quickly and ran into the kitchen, where she saw Berry hitting Mother, and Carrie, with her bloodied mouth and shirt, hitting and punching Berry.

Mother looked over at Sissy and told her to run and get out of there. Sissy was shaking. She was terrified. She wanted to pass out from the sight of the blood on Carrie's mouth, chin, and clothes. But fear set in, and Sissy turned around and ran outside.

She got into her car, closed the door, and cranked up the engine. She started backing up in the driveway. Berry ran outside. He picked up rocks and started throwing them at Sissy's car. Sissy heard the rocks striking the car and looked in the rearview mirror. She saw Berry running toward her, throwing rocks, but she reached the end of the driveway and sped off, leaving Berry at the end of Mother's long driveway, still throwing rocks at her car.

Inside the house, Carrie had helped Mother up off the floor. Mother ran into the living room and grabbed her purse. She looked at Carrie and said, "Listen, we need to be quiet."

They snuck out the back door of the kitchen. Mother grabbed and held Carrie's hand as they crept around the back of the house. They stopped and peeked around the corner of it. As soon as Mother saw Berry walk through the front door, she turned to Carrie and said, "Let's go!" And they made a mad dash to her car. They got into the car, and Mom fumbled with the keys trying to start the engine. Berry ran out of the front door screaming at them. Carrie locked her door on the passenger side. Berry started banging on Mother's car, yelling at them to get out.

Mother finally got the key in and started the engine. She backed the car up, with Berry walking alongside the car and continuing to hit and beat on the car. Mother put the car in drive and tromped on the gas pedal, slinging rocks across the driveway and into the yard.

Sissy was almost to the school, but she stopped and parked at a gas station. She got out of her car and walked over to the pay phone where she called our uncle Tom.

In the meantime, Berry had walked back over to his father's house and had gotten his rifle. He walked back over to Mother's house and climbed the tall pecan tree next to the barn.

Mother and Carrie arrived at Uncle Tom's house where Aunt Carol greeted them with hugs. "Are y'all okay?"

"I am," Mother replied. "But Carrie will need to see a dentist as soon as possible." Mother used Aunt Carol's phone to call Aunt Cassie. Aunt Carol sat down next to Carrie on the couch in the living room. She asked Carrie, "Can I get you anything?" Carrie shook her head no.

Mother reached Aunt Cassie and told her what had happened. Aunt Cassie had a friend who was a dentist, so she gave Mother his name and phone number and told Mother to call right away. "I am going to get Scott to go with me over to your house," Aunt Cassie added. "Tom may need some help dealing with Berry, and I don't want Tom to kill Berry."

"Thank you so much, Cassie. I love you and please be careful," Mother said, as she hung up the phone.

When Aunt Cassie and her boyfriend, Scott, got to Mother's house, Uncle Tom was already there. I arrived shortly after Aunt Cassie and Scott.

My poor Sissy had to board the school bus with all the other cheerleaders and the football team while trying to act like everything was okay. When everyone was loaded on the school bus, it left the school and passed by Mother's house just a couple of minutes after all the police cars had surrounded it.

One of Sissy's best friends was sitting beside her on the school bus. Maxine saw all the police cars surrounding Mother's house. She looked over at Sissy and saw the look of fear and embarrassment on Sissy's face. Maxine put her arm around Sissy and hugged her. Sissy had to see all that and experience it, right before she had to go out onto a football field and act happy and cheer on the football team. Sissy had no idea if Mother and Carrie were okay. She had to wait until she returned home later that night to find out.

Berry stayed in jail for a while after that awful day. Carrie went to my Aunt Cassie's friend the dentist that night; he met my mother and Carrie in his office. He fixed Carrie's front tooth. Mother put the house and land up for sale and sold it. Berry lived with his father next door until his father passed away and Berry's stepmother kicked him out. Berry moved to a small town in north central Texas and lived by himself. He was working one day, doing a service call, while he was still running his father's business. He completed the job and went to the front door and knocked to collect the money from the customer. The customer, a male, told him to wait a minute.

Berry waited just outside the front door, and as he heard the click from the man's rifle, Berry turned around and moved quickly toward his truck. The man opened up the screen door and yelled at Berry, "Hey, don't you want your money?"

Berry turned around, and the man shot him in the abdomen. Berry did not die, but he ended up living the rest of his life with a bag in his gut.

Berry tried a couple of times to reach out to me, Kristine, and Carrie, but it was too late. The damage had been done. We did not want to have anything to do with him, and we didn't. He mailed letters to us, but he did not apologize for any of the things that he had put us through.

Berry died in October 2018. He had bypass surgery and passed away the next day from complications. When I found out about his death, even though I had not seen him or talked to him in many years, I started crying. I was sad. For some reason, I immediately started thinking about the good things that he had done — sometimes. I thought about the times he did try to do something good and be a good father, but those times were few and far between.

When my sister Kristine found out about his death, she was at work and she started crying. As soon as she started crying, she thought to herself, why am I crying? And she stopped. Carrie did not cry at all. Berry's surviving siblings, the very same siblings who chose to never be a part of our lives when we were growing up, did not have a service for Berry. They just had him cremated. Berry had had a very rough childhood too. His father had physically and verbally abused him. Mother always said that Berry was an intelligent man who could have done or been anything that he wanted to do or be, but he had chosen the wrong path.

On the one hand, Berry's story was a sad one, but I still remember, and I also feel, all the terror and fear that we experienced because of his actions. He could have chosen to be a good husband and a good father. But he didn't.

My sisters and I chose to be good people as little girls and as adults. Mother always told us to treat people the way that we wanted to be treated. So, we chose to be nice and good to people. Even though we went through all that horror and terror every time Berry got drunk and beat our mother up, or when the ghost decided to scare us and torment us, we always had hope for a brighter future, faith that we would survive, and our love for one another.

Do I wish every day that things growing up could have been different and much better? You bet I do. But the things that my sisters and I went through and witnessed while growing up made us who we are today. It made us resilient. It made our bond unbreakable. We are stronger together, and nothing can take that away.

ABOUT THE AUTHOR

This book was written to call attention to domestic abuse and the effect it has on small children in particular, as well as adult victims, living in such harsh environments. J.S. Stone wrote this book from her own memories of witnessing violence in the home against her mother. It is her supreme wish that there comes a day when no person feels the fear and first-hand suffering that takes place growing up in a home where random volatile acts take place against beloved family members. *Three Sisters in a Tin House* is her first novel.